Reforming Schools

Reforming Schools

Working within a Progressive Tradition during Conservative Times

Jesse Goodman

Foreword by
Andrew Gitlin

State University
of New York
Press

Published by
State University of New York Press, Albany

For information, address State University of New York Press,
194 Washington Avenue, Suite 305, Albany, NY 12210-2384

Production by Susan Geraghty
Marketing by Susan Petrie

This book was supported in part through the generosity of the Bay and Paul Foundations.

Library of Congress Cataloging-in-Publication Data

Goodman, Jesse, 1948–
  Reforming schools : working within a progressive tradition during
conservative times / Jesse Goodman.
    p. cm.
  Includes bibliographical references and index.
  ISBN 0-7914-6795-3 (alk. paper) — ISBN 0-7914-6796-1 (pbk. : alk.
paper)
    1. School improvement programs—United States. 2. School management
and organization—United States. 3. Curriculum change—United States. I.
Title.

LB2822.82.G67 2006
371.2'00973—dc22

                                                                2005020542

ISBN-13: 978-0-7914-6795-4 (hardcover : alk. paper)
ISBN-13: 978-0-7914-6796-1 (pbk. : alk. paper)

10 9 8 7 6 5 4 3 2 1

This book is dedicated to
B. Robert Tabachnick.

CONTENTS

FOREWORD

The beginning of the twenty-first century is not an encouraging time to be a progressive educator. The conservative restoration (Apple, 2001) with its emphasis on testing, accountability, and nationally directed standards is picking up speed. Teachers, as a consequence, are being deskilled (Apple, 1986; Gitlin, 1983). The problematic relation between culture, curriculum, and schooling is also strengthened as pedagogical relationships between students and teachers are becoming more strained and alienated (Weis and Fine, 1993). And so the query before many of us who take a progressive bent is: What can be done?

Academics, of many stripes, have leaped into the fray to address this query. For some, conservatives, the answer lies in strengthening the conservative restoration by increasing standards, dictating curriculum, and coming down hard on students that don't abide with school norms and dominant forms of socialization (Hirsch, 1988; Ravitch and Finn, 1989). For others, the radical left, the answer lies in taking a macro view of schooling, where schools are placed within a social context such that a good deal of attention is focused on the types of ideological and structural changes that need to occur if education is to become a force in the emancipation or transformation of cultural relations. For those trying to strengthen the conservative restoration it is hard to see how their proposals do more than make an already unequal playing field tilt toward those having the advantages of the "center" (i.e., the symbolic place where communities and cultures gain legitimacy and advantage by helping to form and then embody the types of cultural codes and mores associated with a particular view of expertise, status, value, and success). While this romantic vision of a society lost has some appeal to those cultural groups trying to maintain and increase the snug fit between schooling and dominant culture, a broader view of the issue, especially when looked at from the point of view of cultural groups typically disenfranchised by schooling, indicates that the reinforcement of the conservative restoration will, at best, legitimate Seymour Sarason's refrain (1971) that the more things change the more they stay the same. Conversely, the problem for the radical left is not about the lack of change proposed or even its potential to alter the nature of schooling and its relation to culture but rather how to implement the broadly conceptualized recommendations within the limitations and constraints currently embodied within schooling. It is one thing to propose a critical pedagogy or critical literacy (Freire, 1993), and another to figure out how to utilize such an approach with an alienated teaching faculty who already feel overwhelmed by the increasing demands of testing and standardization. Understanding how the dominant images of society are reproduced within a schooling context, how the curriculum reflects an Anglo bias is different from considering how to put into place reforms or even transformations that take these understandings and place them within a context where teachers often have little autonomy in terms of the curriculum and content they teach.

Where my bias is clearly on the side of those trying to create a more level playing field that significantly transforms the relation between schooling and culture, *only* producing more of the same types of texts, what might be called terrain adjusters (i.e., they adjust our understanding of the terrain known as schooling), may be limited in moving us in a direction that could broadly be termed progressive. And thus the rub is that not only are there limited options, but more importantly a third alternative is surely a "risky business." Why, you ask? It is risky because as soon as one moves toward the practical, toward a contextual notion of reform, toward working within the boundaries of the established limits of schooling, one is leaving the community codes of the radical left and inching toward a community that the left despises almost as much as the conservatives—the liberal community with its focus on individualism and working within established institutional structures. It takes great courage, therefore, and a lack of care for one's standing within the established leftist community, to move beyond the boundaries of this progressive group of scholars. This is not to suggest that doing so will necessarily produce something of added value. And it is not to suggest that the left itself is flawed. Rather, I want to suggest, that we shouldn't be surprised that, as is true of most communities, there is a type of disciplinary work occurring within the leftist community that limits the types of questions and answers proposed to our most pressing educational questions. And therefore it is important to see those community codes and, where deemed desirable, to move beyond them.

And yet, it the midst of this pessimistic framework, comes a book that breaks the mold. *Reforming Schools* by Jesse Goodman takes on both the conservatives and the radical left (for different reasons, mind you) and proposes an historical, contextual approach to democratic reform that is decidedly alternative to many of the proposals outlined by the leftist community as well as the proposals coming from those who want to strengthen the conservative restoration. The "middle ground theory" articulated in this text is only one of the contributions of this important book. Another contribution is the language used and the linkage of theory and practice.

In recent years, great strides have been made concerning the debate known in some circles as the politics of clarity (Giroux, 1995). On one side of this debate are those who believe that writing in a clear style has the unintended consequence of representing theories in familiar ways that pulls those theories and proposals back toward the center—the space of dominant interests. In contrast, there are those who argue that writing which is less jargonistic and is clear, opens texts to a wider audience and allows groups to enter debates that normally would be closed to those without the specialized training to wade through complex difficult texts. My take on this debate is that we (all those on the left) should not limit ourselves to disciplinary action that creates firm and rigid boundaries on our community. In contrast, I would suggest there is room for all types of representations that might tie in with various audiences and still provide innovative alternative theories and conceptualizations. What I see, in the Goodman text, is again a third alternative. While it is true that there are leftist texts that are clear and accessible and those that are complex and jargonistic, rarely are there texts that are conceptually rich, practical and accessible. Goodman has produced such a text. In doing so, Goodman has also accomplished something equally rare. As opposed to thinking about how to move from an intellectual terrain, terrain-adjuster perspective, with its focus on understanding to a practical orientation, Goodman is in the schools trying to make the everyday world problematic (Smith, 1987). As such, he develops his understanding not from the reified air of an intellectual terrain adjustor but rather from the messy earth of someone working on the front lines of schooling. Understanding emerges from intervention not solely from a conceptual framework of understanding that is applied to practice. Again, this is not to say that this interventionist approach is right or better, but rather that we need many understandings of schooling from all sorts of differing angles and Goodman provides a text, in an alternative key, that is represented in a way that allows many audiences to interact with this conceptually rich and practical text. With this overview in mind, I would like to turn now to some of the more specific arguments found in the Goodman text and their relation to the field of education in general.

Goodman begins his adventure into educational reform by identifying a problem—the lack of focus and integration of a potential coalition of progressive educators. There can be little doubt that Goodman is interested in furthering (the coalition already is partially formed) such a coalition—a coalition that not only opposes the conservative restoration but, as importantly, furthers a democratic orientation to social justice. For Goodman, the coalition he desires has been somewhat constrained by divisions that ignore and undervalue commonalities across differing communities. In particular, his target (this may be too strong a word) is the academic left with its emphasis on class and Marxist theories. From Goodman's point of view, these political scholars have the bounds of their community (they impose discipline by giving priority to the query: Who is a real Leftist?) too narrowly set and as a consequence have not been able to link up with liberals and other humanitarians that, in fact, might and probably would fight for the general goal of social justice. Goodman seeks to reset those bounds so that liberals (at least some that hold onto the historic roots of liberalism) and leftists come together in such a way that fosters a new politics, which he names the "reformist left."

By linking these communities together (liberal or reformist and left) Goodman is trying to confront the status quo—in the sense of challenging the left and liberals to work together to further democratic goals and importantly make a difference at the level of practice. In many ways, the problematic that Goodman addresses harkens back to the 1960s and the debates raging within the group known as Students for a Democratic Society (SDS). Within this group were liberals, Marxists, and even Buddhists (the Beats). And as is true today, this type of progressive coalition did not necessarily see eye to eye. What Gitlin (1987) makes clear in his accounting of events relating to the early establishment of SDS is that liberals were often segregated from the radical left and when an individual, especially a liberal, tried to cross over to the radical left, there were great debates on the legitimacy of the qualifications of this individual to pass the muster of being a true leftist. On the other hand, both leftists and liberals wanted to separate themselves from the beat generation—the Buddhists who were most interested in finding enlightenment through meditation. While clearly the times are a changin' and have changed, in some ways the left is still, and has always been, plagued with issues relating to community boundaries. In particular, as is true today, in the 1960s potential coalitions of a progressive nature were fractured so that political action was truncated and made less of a difference than might have been the case. And it is this issue of making a difference, a progressive difference, that is at the heart of Goodman's text and his proposals.

What Goodman is trying to do in this regard, is reconfigure coalition building by having progressives look at the coalition not in terms of where communities differ but what it would take to make a difference in a school and for the students in that particular school. Whether Goodman has it right is not clear to me, what is clear is that he is addressing reform in a way that many others have not and is asking questions that will be central to any movement that wants to move beyond the status quo. As opposed to many reform scholars that simply try to figure out the best way to engineer an effective approach to reform (see Fullan, 1993), Goodman is trying to figure out what it would take to further the process of reform that has a defined and articulated purpose. Further, as opposed to reform scholars that have focused their attention on developing models of teacher development and conceptual approaches to collaboration (Hargreaves, 1994), Goodman tries to understand development and collaboration within an interventionist perspective that takes into account limited teacher autonomy as well as historic divisions between parents, students, and teachers, and the local school district office. Goodman not only provides such a contextual point of view and set of practices, but he does so in an openly ideological manner (Lather, 1986) that does not separate out purpose and desire from reform possibilities and orientations.

While Goodman's argument may be flawed, in the sense that all arguments are flawed if looked at over time and community orientation, he nevertheless makes a vital, central contribution to debates about schooling by directing our attention to the issue of coalition-building and the role it might play in fostering reform and a more democratic type of schooling that enhances human dignity, respect, and value for all.

Reforming schools, however, does not simply utilize a standard view of democracy and insert it into its proposals. Instead, Goodman works from practice and academic texts to develop a view of a critical, social, and liberal democracy. Democracy, within this conception, is connected to a form of pragmatism that directs our attention to the social aspects of life. By doing so, not only does Goodman's democracy embrace human diversity and self-actualization, but reflects the politics of recognition committed to inclusion, social justice, and the fortification of a collective "we" identity. At first blush, what is apparent in this view of democracy is that it reflects what is clearly a focus of the book—working across differences. By associating democracy with pragmatism, self-actualization, social justice, and a collective "we," Goodman is linking this concept of democracy to liberal and radical traditions such that it is possible to form coalitions that work across historic differences (i.e., the left and liberals). But Goodman does not stop there, as previously mentioned, he then takes this concept of democracy and links it to his work at the Harmony Education Center (in Bloomington, Indiana) and shows how his view of democracy is both implemented and mediated as it is put into practice. While the details of this implementation are quite important, for the purposes of this foreword, what is telling is that Goodman is providing the reader with a type of methodology on how to think about the relation between educational reform and the movement of society toward a more critical, social, and liberal democracy. Not only does he ask unique questions such as those focusing on the relation between coalition-building and reform, but he links reform to purpose and desire, thereby avoiding an engineering approach, and develops his conceptual framework (like his concept of democracy) from an interaction between academic texts and interventionist practices. As such, his view of democracy changes, as does its meaning, as the possibilities and limits within an institution change over time. From Goodman's perspective, democracy is a "moving concept," not a fixed stable view that can simply be placed into any context at any time. In my view, this is a major contribution to the literature because many analyses of democracy are quite stable, posing one view over another (Pateman, 1970). While this stable approach is helpful, in the final analysis democracy requires change and alterations within changing contexts and ideological orientations. By modeling this "moving view" of what democracy means, Goodman has cleared a path for others to not only consider purpose, desire, and reform, but to do so in a way that allows for a congruency between the values of democracy and the values of the reform movement. While it is likely we might quibble with any number of details within Goodman's proposals (and I believe he would want you to), I hope you will look carefully at the unique questions he asks about reform as well as how his purposes and desires for reform (e.g., critical, social, liberal democracy) are developed.

With this framework for the book in place, the major work of the text is just starting. That work includes learning what educational reform geared toward a more comprehensive democracy means when put into practice. The first issue of concern identified is that of autonomy. I find the focus on autonomy refreshing and intriguing. The left, in particular, has focused a great deal of their scholarship on the issue of control. What the left has done quite expertly is to show how control can be direct, technical, and bureaucratic (Edwards, 1979). In the last few decades, this progressive group of scholars has also shown how even structural constraints do not determine behavior, relations, and ideological formations—there is always a degree of relative autonomy (Apple, 1986). While this has provided a major step forward in terms of understanding reform, what has been often overlooked is what it would mean to cultivate autonomy (in some ways, the other pole of control) as an a priori requirement of reform and democracy. And it is this tack that Goodman takes. He sets the stage to understand the pragmatic constraints and possibilities of having autonomy provide a foundation for reform and democracy in school settings. And in my view this makes a great deal of sense. For if democracy is to be about self-actualization, the politics of recognition, and so forth, it is difficult to see how this might come into practice unless, in a real sense, teachers, students, and parents had some autonomy to make decisions that they felt would be helpful and educative for all cultures within the corridors of schooling. What is so refreshing and unique about Goodman's work with autonomy, is that it is not put forward as a seamless concept that works in all and any circumstances. Goodman shows the successes and the limitations of putting democracy, and specifically autonomy, into place within a school setting.

With this complex and central view of autonomy in place, Goodman sets his sights on two related issues of importance when thinking about school reform and democracy—these are voice and working through conflict. Within the leftist literature there has been no lack of discussion about voice. Some see voice in cultural terms, such as providing counter stories to the dominant views that saturate the airways. Others see voice as the ability to allow those traditionally silenced to speak their mind and teach us through their experiential and conceptual knowledge about issues of oppression and marginalization. Again, these views are extremely important and helpful in any number of ways. However, they do tend to separate out a conception of voice from what might be called the pragmatics of voice (by this I mean how voice can make a difference at the level of practice). What is unique about Goodman's view is that voice is thought of in pragmatic terms such that it is not separated from the issue of decision making. In practice, at the Harmony Education Center, what voice means is having a say in a particular decision, a decision made through consensus. Yes, questions can and should be raised about the problems of using consensus as a mode of decision making. Nevertheless, what is telling about Goodman's proposal is that he is connecting voice to decision making and ultimately to issues of autonomy. As I was reading this part of the text, I kept thinking how this is a critical part of our understanding of reform—how we can take a concept like voice and actually see what the concept looks like as it is put into practice—and not just any practice but a set of practices that push us toward the ambition of democratic schooling and living. This is not only unique in the academic literature, but provides a range of possibilities and constraints that will have to be looked at carefully as one moves forward toward implementing a reform that in one sense or another, could be termed progressive.

The second issue related to the foundation of autonomy is the issue of conflict. Conflict, has been a central theme within leftist educational literature. In particular, what this literature claims, quite rightly in my view, is that the shunning of conflict has a indirect and at times direct impact at fortifying the status quo. Since the left sees the status quo as embedded with inequities, this aspect of social life and society in general must be challenged. One way to challenge the status quo is to view conflict as a part of the change process that must be acknowledged and in certain circumstances embraced. So, when conflict arose within the schools where Harmony Educational Center worked, the change agents, including Goodman, didn't sweep this issue under the rug, but took the bold and educative move of bringing all the school-based groups together and having a series of conversations about conflict. As was true of other issues discussed in this text, at times these discussions focused on academic texts and what they had to say, and at other times the conversations emerged from the pragmatics of a school set upon a course to foster a more critical, social, liberal democracy in our society. This type of linkage of text and pragmatics, is not only unique but importantly provides an alternative source of knowledge that expands our horizons in thinking through conflict and especially the issue of how to deal with conflict so that the culture of the school does not disintegrate but rather becomes a source for productive and progressive change within the context of a democratic ethos.

The concluding section of the book returns the reader to the beginning— to the realities of a conservative restoration. Of course, these realities are not simply accepted. Rather, data are provided on what can be done to challenge the way the conservative agenda infiltrates the classroom. Teaching to the marketplace and high-stakes testing are a few of the topics discussed. What is intriguing about this discussion, and linked with the entire theme of the text, is that high-stakes testing, for example, is not simply criticized nor is it validated. Instead, there is an ongoing discussion on what can and should be done when testing confronts autonomy, voice, and all the other related aspects of fostering reform geared toward democracy. This kind of discussion helps flesh out a hopeful sense of what can be done when progressive reform meets the conservative restoration as embodied within the institution of schooling.

I have often felt that our views of education are best seen within the details of the argument. With the publication of *Reforming Schools*, I can now see that something more is needed. Goodman's text does provide detail, but as importantly he asks questions, and develops concepts that have often been overlooked in the academic literature. As you read this text, therefore, I not only encourage you to decide where you disagree and agree, but also to look at the "method," if you will, that underlies this text. This method can be applied to your context and help you see what makes a difference in the lives of students. This method connects change with desire and a type of humanism that focuses on our connections and a common goal: human respect, recognition, and lives that are fully self-actualized.

ANDREW GITLIN
UNIVERSITY OF GEORGIA

PREFACE

Efforts to reform schools are intimately rooted in the conscious and/or sub-conscious visions of what one might consider to be a "good society." As mentioned in the first chapter, this book represents an effort to create images and discuss issues of school reform that are contextualized within a progressive history of the United States. Given the failures of twentieth century socialist experiments and the unfortunate shift of the United States towards conservative ideology during the last twenty to thirty years, the development of a progressive vision is crucial. Without this historical orientation, it is far too easy for progressive-thinking educators, scholars, and other cultural workers to become overly discouraged in light of recent developments, and thus withdraw from involvement in our schools and other important realms (e.g., economics, politics, media, religion) of society. As discussed in the second chapter, this book suggests that school reform efforts are best conceptualized within a larger effort to create a more critical, social, liberal democracy.

Since this book is concerned with the interaction of both social theory and the lived experience of actual work in school reform, it may appeal to people with different interests. As a result, individual readers may wish to approach the book differently. Those who want to be more fully informed about this author's vision of progressive history, and its relationship to school reform will most likely want to read the book from beginning to end in the order that it is written. Those who are particularly interested in the lived experiences of school reform efforts and lessons learned from these experiences may wish to begin their reading with chapters 3–6, and then after reading these chapters, if the reader is interested in placing this work into a more comprehensive theoretical and historical context, s/he should consider reading the first two chapters.

Some might argue that discussing the lived experiences of progressive school reformers (chapters 3–6) within a reading of western history (chapters 1–2) is a bit schizophrenic. To some degree, this concern is valid. However, as school reformers, our work has been significantly influenced by this reading of history, and an understanding of our work would be incomplete without this historical context. Others might question if our experiences in a relatively small number of schools can really offer insights useful to the vast majority of school reformers who might find themselves in very different situations. Of course, we are not in a position to answer this question. Nevertheless, it is important to remember that if we are ever going to substantively alter the current organization of and practices in schools, then it makes sense to take a careful look at various efforts toward these goals. Only by comprehending a diversity of approaches can we learn from each other. What is being suggested is that we can learn as much, if not more, from carefully examining what happens in unique settings as we can from the generalized norm. The creative challenge for the reader of this book is to vicariously apply what s/he has read to his/her own specific set of circumstances, be that of a single school reformer, an administrator who desires to become a transformative leader and thus move beyond the mere management of a school or district, a group of teachers in a school who might wish to create a "school within a school," or scholars who are interested in studying and/or assisting those educators involved in the reform of conventional schooling in our society.

Of course, no book is ever written by one individual. As I have indicated in a footnote on the first page of each chapter, several key individuals helped me compose the ideas found within this manuscript. In addition, much of the analysis for the first two chapters emerged from a study group I organized that included the following individuals: Jim Ansaldo, Jeffery Woods, Joanne Turk, Karen Grady, Mary Bourke, Ruth Nieboer, Sally Hood, and Becky McGraw. Other colleagues who have provided feedback along the way include: Wendy Walter-Bailey, Tom Kelly, Andrew Gitlin, and Lynne Boyle-Baise. This book could never have been completed without the help of my wife, Dona Naeser. Although she did not participate in its actual composition, I would never have had the time to do this scholarship if she had not been my willing partner in life and in raising our children.

As is common in our occupation, many of the ideas (or versions thereof) found in this book were previously published in the following manuscripts:

Goodman, J. (1994). External change agents and grassroots school reform: Reflections from the field. *Journal of Curriculum and Supervision*, 9 (2), 113–135.

Goodman, J. (1994). Circles of democracy: A school's internal governance. *New Education*, 16 (2), 3–23. Reprinted in J. Zajda, K Bacchus, and N. Kach (Eds.), *Excellence and quality in education*, 159–183. Albert Park, Australia: James Nicholas Publishers, 1995.

Goodman, J. (1996). Artifacts of change: An archaeology of school-based educational reform. *Interchange: A Quarterly Review of Education*, 27 (3–4), 279–312.

Goodman, J. and Kuzmic, J. (1997). Bringing progressive education into conventional schools: Theoretical and practical implications. *Theory Into Practice*, 36 (2), 79–86.

Goodman, J., Baron, D. and Myers, C. (1999). The local politics of educational reform: Issues of school autonomy. *Research for Educational Reform*, 4 (2), 22–49.

Goodman, J., Baron, D., and Myers, C. (2001). Bringing democracy to the occupational life of educators: Constructing a foundation for school-based reform. *International Journal of Educational Leadership*, 4 (1), 57–86.

Goodman, J., Baron, D., and Myers, C. (2001). Talking back to the neo-liberal agenda from the ground floor: School-based reform discourses in difficult times. *International Journal of Educology*, 12–15 (1), 1–38.

Goodman, J., Baron, D., and Myers, C. (2005). Constructing a democratic foundation for school-based reform: The local politics of school autonomy and internal governance. In F. English (Ed.), *Handbook of educational leadership*. New York: Sage Press.

Finally, I dedicate this book to B. Robert Tabachnick, my academic mentor and friend. Not only did he support and encourage my work as a young scholar, but he was also instrumental in the development of my thinking as well as a model of one who is always in search for ideas that help us, as a species, become more alive and curious about the world into which we are born.

CHAPTER 1

The Times in Which We Work:
The Conservative Restoration

During the last twenty-five to thirty years a resurgence of conservative ideology has swept across our schools and society. This latest "conservative restoration" began within the political realm of society with such events as the signing of civil rights and voting rights laws in 1964, implementation of Richard Nixon's "southern strategy" that successfully incorporated the Dixiecrats into the Republican Party, the subsequent election of Ronald Reagan, which in turn set the stage for the "dixification" of the U.S. economy and culture (Cummings, 1998), and the election of a fundamentalist Christian president. As leftist, school reformers, we are acutely aware of the impact this conservative resurgence has had (and is having) on the education of our children. As Apple (2001) and others (e.g., Miller, 1995) have discussed, the ramifications of this restoration include (among other things): public-supported vouchers for children going to private schools, high-stakes testing, legislation of curriculum content (i.e., standards), emphasis on drilling and memorization, internal racial segregation through tracking, the deskilling of teachers, and a deepening of "savage inequalities" related to the inequitable resources provided to children of wealthy versus those to impoverished children (Kozol, 1992). During the last dozen years, we have studied and worked with administrators, teachers, parents, and students to minimize the negative consequences of this ideological shift in our society and to promote an alternative orientation to school reform rooted in a tradition of leftist reformism. For the purposes of this book, the reformist left refers to a purposefully broad ideological range of both sociopolitical and educational ideas that are rooted in American pragmatism[1] within intellectual discourses (e.g., Barber, 1998; Dewey, 1920; Fraser, 1997; Galston, 2002; Menand, 2001; Rawls, 2001; Rorty, 1989, 1998) and progressivism within the British (e.g., Giddens, 2003; Lawson and Sherlock, 2001) and U.S. (e.g., Kloppenberg, 1986; Sklar, 1988; Wiebe, 1967) political discourses. Unlike radical leftists scholars and educators (e.g., Brosio, 2004; McLaren, 2000; Rikowski, 1996; Wood and Foster, 1997) who seek to destroy capitalism, otherize the bourgeoisie, discount the importance of representative democracy,

*Thanks to Linda Holloway for her assistance with this chapter.

1

and have an unfortunate tendency to blame the United States for nearly every problem in the world today, reform leftists seek to authentically alter the institutions and ideology that we have inherited from our ancestors, to substantively address the numerous "problems of (wo)men" (Dewey, 1946 [1929]) found within the various realms or spheres of our society (e.g., economic, political, media, religious, educational, military), and promote reciprocal and equitable international relationships with other societies that currently exist upon this planet we share. Aronson (1992, p. 38) noted that despite its ideological nuances, reform leftists have been drawn together

> around four rubrics: (a) we have sought greater equality and human dignity; (b) we have struggled for expanding and deepening the meanings of democracy; (c) we have been a force for social responsibility and solidarity; and (d) we have sought the expansion of and realization of human rights.

Reform leftists in the United States have been associated with attempts to make our democracy more inclusive, advocate for those who are economically marginalized, foster greater awareness of and respect for all citizens and their diverse ancestral heritages, promote policies of equitable access to traditionally powerful realms of our society (e.g., government, business, media services, religion, education), advocate for the secularization of public life, support the development of a prosperous and ecologically sustainable economy, defend individual rights and privacy, and speak out against colonialism and imperialism. Rorty (1989, p. xv), borrowing from the thinking of Judith Shklar, puts it succinctly where he states that reform leftists "are the people who think that cruelty is the worst thing we [humans] do." He goes on to suggest that humiliation is the ultimate cruelty, and notes the importance reform leftists have given to the ideals of universal, human dignity. In particular, reform leftists have been at the forefront of calling attention to and resisting all forms of "otherization" that occur within a given polity.[2]

Just prior to the conservative restoration, several progressive educational critiques, practices, and policies gained momentum in the United States. During the 1960s and 1970s, books such as *Compulsory Mis-education* (Goodman, 1964), *36 Children* (Kohl, 1967), *Death at an Early Age* (Kozol, 1967), *Crisis in the Classroom* (Silberman, 1970), *How Children Learn* (Holt, 1967), and *Teaching as a Subversive Activity* (Postman and Weingartner, 1969) among others called attention to the dismal state of intellectual activity, racism, and humiliation found within many of our schools (particularly those located in high poverty areas), and offered ideas to make the education of *all* our children (regardless of their wealth, ancestral heritage, or academic talents) and their teachers more personally meaningful, culturally relevant, politically sensitive, inclusive, and intellectually stimulating.

However, these ideas, concerns, and efforts were significantly curtailed after the publication of *A Nation at Risk*. As Berlinger and Biddle (1995) cogently point out, in spite of the fact that this report was filled with misinformation, inaccurate analyses, and war-like jargon pointed against teachers who had little to do with the most significant failings of schools at the time, it initiated a twenty-plus-year conservative attack on progressive efforts to educate the children of our nation. Although the conservative restoration significantly reversed the public orientation towards the schooling of our children, it has not put the efforts of many leftist educators, scholars, and other cultural workers to a complete halt. How have we, as leftist school reformers, struggled to improve the education of our children in light of this conservative resurgence in our society and schools? How have we worked with individual schools, as well as with groups of teachers, parents, administrators, and others from around the country to resist the ramifications of the now fully established conservative schooling of our children and foster progressive ideas and practices in light of the right's current power in this country?

In response to these questions, this book will present an analytical portrayal of our work at the Harmony Education Center (HEC). HEC was founded in 1990 as a collaboration between Harmony School (Goodman, 1992), an independent school created in 1974 (see chapter 2), and Indiana University. However, prior to describing this center in more detail and analytically exploring its work, we believe it necessary to examine more fully, as the chapter's title suggests, the times in which we work. From our perspective, one of the major weaknesses of progressive citizens in our society is their lack of historical understanding. HEC was created within a particular understanding of the temporal landscape we inherited, and thus an explication of this understanding is valuable to other educators and critics who wish to comprehend "where we are coming from." In response, this chapter will first provide a brief review of the contemporary history from which this conservative restoration emerged during the last two decades of the twentieth century. Second, we utilize a significant variation of Marx's class analysis to provide one way of understanding why this restoration is currently so powerful within the United States. This analysis has furnished us with a useful lens through which we can comprehend the struggles facing leftist school reformers and educational scholars, today and in the future.

THE CONSERVATIVE RESTORATION

Space does not allow for, nor is it necessary to present, a comprehensive review of the conservative ideology, policies, and practices that have swept our country during the last thirty years as others have already explored this phenomenon from several perspectives as it has been manifested within education and other realms of society (e.g., Apple, 2001; Barber, 1998; Blau, 1999; Brock, 2001; MacEwan, 1999; Shor, 1992; Sunstein, 1997; Wallerstein, 1995). Nevertheless, in order to set the context of our analytical portrayal, it is useful to briefly explore this recent ideological phenomenon. We begin with a review of contemporary history, followed by an examination of the power that lies behind this conservative thinking in the United States, and a review of some of its educational ramifications.

Contemporary Historical Overview

The United States has always been a relatively conservative nation. Its creation at the end of the eighteenth century represented the first effort in the West to establish a nation state solely in the tradition of what was then called European liberalism. As we have previously explored (Goodman, 1992), the United States is a nation deeply rooted in individualism, capitalism, and Christianity. However, as Cummings (1998) noted, throughout most of the twentieth century with the exception of the first conservative restoration that took place during the 1920s, this nation's deeply held commitment to classical liberalism began to erode. It is reasonable to trace this second conservative restoration that began in the latter part of the twentieth century, in part, to the relatively modest successes of this erosion brought about by various progressive campaigns. Throughout the last century, these leftist struggles made significant changes in a wide range of societal realms (e.g., economic, political, educational, media, military) of our country. Many of the benefits that emerged from this leftist agitation are unfortunately, today, taken for granted, which has left them vulnerable to successful attacks in our current socio-political climate. It is important to remember that prior to the twentieth century there was little or no government regulation over business, banking, or monetary activities (e.g., antimonopoly laws, Federal Reserve Board, Securities and Exchange Commission); recognition of or laws protecting labor unions (the vast majority of workers remained impoverished), regulation of weekly work hours (60-hour work weeks were common) or prohibitions of child labor; as well as public support for education; income assistance (e.g., social security, medicaid, medicare, minimum wage laws, welfare) or other forms of income redistribution such as a progressive income tax or estate taxes; not to mention more recent successful struggles for civil and gender rights, rights of personal privacy, freedom of information, and election reforms that modestly (and temporarily) minimize the corrupting influence of money in politics. In general, the twentieth century brought about a significant change in the social, economic, and political thinking of Americans, or what conservatives like to critique as the "era of big government" (Willis, 1999). Although relatively temperate by radical leftist standards, these alterations in the United States have been deeply troubling to conservatives who have, in the last three decades, successfully halted the leftist momentum of the nation. Their determination to regain their lost hegemony was given an unforseen augmentation by the radicalization of the left that took place in the United States (and other Western countries) during the 1960s and 1970s.

It is useful to remember that most of the leftist campaigns (e.g., the women's suffrage and liberation movements, the public education movement, the labor and antitrust movements, the civil rights movement, the ecology movement, the health and consumer safety movement, the antiwar movement) in the United States during the nineteenth and twentieth centuries presented their efforts within a context of the national narrative (e.g., Banaszak, 1996; Buechler, 2000; Fox, 1986; Gourley, 1999; Gottlieb, 2005; Himmelberg, 1994; Katz, 1968; Kessler-Harris, 2001; Le Blanc, 1999; Lichtenstein, 2002; Olson, 2001; Rosen, 2001; Schneirov, 1998; Sklar, 1988; Storrs, 2000). That is, prior to the late 1960s, these leftist movements were, for the most part, advocated within a discourse of improving the state of the union, or as the Constitution states, the promotion of the "general welfare" of the people. Specifically, these movements were generated within a national narrative of making the United States a more democratic, open, inclusive, prosperous, ecological, and socially just society. The goal was to improve upon, rather than destroy, the society as it existed. As several scholars have noted (e.g., Elbaum, 2002; Hook, 1975; Gitlin, 1987; Isserman and Kazin, 2000; Kurlansky, 2004; Rorty, 1998), the 1960s "new left" in the United States became radicalized, sparked by the government's unjustified prosecution of the Vietnam War (Ellsberg, 2002) and the pent-up rage among young African Americans that was released in the inner cities in response to our country's racism. As college students began to re-examine our country's history (e.g., its genocide of American Indians, oppression of both voluntary and involuntary immigrants and women, unjustifiable wars against Mexico and Spain, its active support of neofascist dictatorships in many parts of Latin America and Asia), they became deeply disillusioned, having grown up on myths about the United States being the "land of the free" and champion of the "oppressed and dispossessed." As a result, many on the new left became radicalized, believing that the country was totally corrupt, evil, and beyond repair. From the perspective of these radicalized leftists, notions such as social justice, democracy, emancipation, liberation, and freedom were antithetical to the polity of the United States. Many turned (including, for a time, the author of this book) to Marxist/Leninism choosing to ignore the basic flaws in Marx's analyses of capitalism and the inherent oppression built into his and Lenin's visions of how to bring about and build a "socialist society" (e.g., Avrich, 1970; Burgler, 1990; Courtois et al., 1999; Fernández, 2000; Gouldner, 1979, 1980; Hook, 1975; Hosking, 1985; Kornai, 1992; Leder, 2001; Lovell, 1988; Meredith, 2002; Pipes, 1990, 1995) or blaming these flaws and the embedded oppression of Marxist theory on Stalin (e.g., Dunayevskaya, 1992; Mandel, 1973; Marcuse, 1985[1958]; Trotsky, 1972 [1937]). During these times, it became popular among the new left to believe that building a humane society would be impossible until capitalism (especially in the United States) was obliterated.[3] Radical leftists tried to convince Americans that nearly everything about the United States was deprived of nobility, reeked of greed, and lacked any authentic commitment to the common good. No longer was it enough to reform our country, now it must be destroyed for the benefit of humanity and the environment. As the popularity of radicalism died, many who maintained a commitment to radical leftist political and economic perspectives sought and obtained positions in universities given these institution's historical commitment to critical inquiry, intellectual study, and open discourse.[4]

Unfortunately, by 1980, the unforeseen consequences of this leftist radicalization were ready to leap upon our country. In particular, this radicalization deeply alienated the electorate in the United States. Like every other polity on earth, the United States has a sordid history and continues to pursue policies that, from a leftist perspective, should cause shame in our collective consciousness. However, the radical left completely discounted that this same nation has, to a certain degree and throughout its history, supported efforts to make life on this planet more democratic, socially just, and equitable. Rorty (1998) notes that modern nation states (i.e., their economic, political, cultural systems) are best viewed as complex, collective subjectivities that reflect a wide range of both humane and inhumane activities, values, ideas, and policies. By focusing only on those aspects of the United States that illuminated the latter, and completely discounting the nation's efforts at the former, the radical left alienated many who might otherwise be sympathetic to our progressive history as a nation (Wolfe, 1998). Most disturbing was the ability of conservative politicians and intellectuals to link the reform-leftist tradition in the United States to the radical leftists of the 1960s and 1970s. Few on the left who were adults then can forget Reagan's success at scorning the term "liberal." While the radical left had already weakened this concept by chiding those who would dare called themselves "liberal" for not being radical enough, Reagan was able to successfully demonize the term and those associated with it. His election paved the way for the eventual ascendency of conservatives in both houses of Congress, but more importantly, was his success at fundamentally shifting the ideological orientation of the country away from the reform-leftist agenda, not only within politics, but in nearly every sphere of society (e.g., media, business, education, religion).

The conservative restoration represents the popularity of particular values and ideas within the United States (and other nations) that include (among others): an expansion of capitalist, industrial production around the world, the stimulation and utilization of scientific and technological knowledge and products within Western and Pacific Rim nations, an increased distrust in government regulation of business and publicly funded social justice activities (including education) resulting in a push for budget cuts and privatization of these programs, and an intrusion into the private lives of individuals based upon Christian values. One does not need to be a scholar to recognize the ways in which the restoration of conservative ideas have been manifested within the United States during the last three decades. Perhaps most obvious has been the proliferation of conservative success in state and national elections. Political ideas, policies, and officials that used to be considered "moderate" or "centrist" are now considered "liberal" (e.g., Easton, 2000, Wallerstein, 1995). Other examples of this restoration include: the rise of conservative and fundamentalist, Christian talk radio such as Rush Limbaugh, Oliver North, Gordan Liddy, and Dr. Laura and conservative television networks such as *Fox News* and shows such as *The O'Rielly Factor*, *Hannity and Colmes*, and *Scarborough Country* (Andersen, 1995; Durham and Kellner, 2001), the establishment of numerous well-funded, conservative "think tanks" and institutions such as the Heritage Foundation, John Olin Foundation, Hudson Institute, American Enterprise Institute, and Free Congress Foundation (Stefancic and Delgado, 1996), and the public promotion of conservative intellectuals such as Milton Friedman, William Bennett, and Diane Ravich. Although the effort to globalize (modernize) the world economy, telecommunication, and transportation has been in active operation since the end of World War II as a way of preventing wars by intermeshing the world's economies together, the conservative restoration has successfully pushed (some would charge "forced") for the adoption in "third world" societies of *laissez-faire* rather than for the carefully regulated (by a democratically elected government) capitalism that proved so successful in post-World War II Europe, the United States, and the Pacific Rim countries (e.g., Ambrose, 1971; Barber, 1995; Friedman, 1999; Korten, 1998; Soros, 2002).

Although the election of Clinton was able to temporarily arrest the conservative restoration and succeeded in putting together a relatively mild reformist agenda (e.g., high employment; modest gains in income; more equitable distribution of wealth, less crime, reduction of racism; greater prosperity; foreign policy based upon internationalist cooperation rather than unilateralism; more support for the social needs of marginalized citizens; celebration of our ethnic, racial, gender, and sexual diversity; and greater inclusivity) palatable to the electorate, the initial "election" (and re-election) of George W. Bush and subsequent focus on national safety from external attacks in light of 9/11 has significantly dampened and has reversed many of Clinton's modest successes. However, these manifestations of the conservative coalition do not illuminate the source of its power. Although the distribution of power is labyrinthine in highly complex societies such as the United States, it is important for the purposes of understanding the times in which we work to briefly explore the unique congregation that serves the engine behind this resurgence of conservative ideas, policies, and practices.

THE CONSERVATIVE COALITION:
A NEO-CLASS ANALYSIS

As previously mentioned, to gain an understanding of the power behind the conservative restoration we utilize a substantively altered notion of class analysis. Although certainly not the only lens one can use to gain insight into the power dynamics of a given society, it does offer a particularly compelling way to think about this phenomenon. However, due to the liberties we have taken with Marx's analysis, it is necessary to articulate our departure from its common conceptualization.

Economic Structuralism

Our first point of departure from Marx's understanding of the way power is distributed in modern society concerns his assertion that power is based upon a society's economic structure. In light of history, it seems clear that Marx was mistaken (reductionist) in his contention that all other aspects of society such as the political and legal systems, education, the media, popular entertainment, the arts, and religion are merely epiphenomenal to its economic "base." Both contemporary Marxists and reform leftists assume that the structure of modern society and thus the distribution of power within it is more complex than advocated in Marx's *Das Kapital* (e.g., Bell, 1973; Gramsci, 1971; Habermas, 1975; Jay, 1973). However, some Marxists (e.g., Althusser, 1972; Aronowitz, 1992; Cohen, 1995) and Marxist educational scholars (e.g., Allman, 2001; Brosio, 2004, McLaren, 2000; Rikowski, 1996) have held on to a milder form of economic determinism referred to as "relative economic autonomy." Although economic structure is not viewed as omnipotent, it is considered, in nearly every case, to be the most powerful societal force "in the last instance" or "in the final analysis" (Hunt, 1992, p. 52). In our analysis, the economic realm is a significant center of power in all known cultures; however, the economy is only one of several societal realms (e.g., political, media, religious, education, legal) among which power is dispersed and manifested. After all, in theocracies such as the one that currently exists in Iran, the economic realm of society, while powerful, is subservient to the religious sphere in this country. In modern, capitalist societies with a functioning liberal democracy such as the United States, Japan, Australia, Taiwan, South Korea, and Western Europe, these different realms (and the people who work primarily within them) compete with each other for dominance over the culture as a whole.

Most importantly, the structures within a given society and power that is invested in each of them are dynamic, not static. From our perspective, there is no ultimate, architectonic foundation to society through which power is manifested. Depending upon unique, contingent events, and as a society becomes more densely populated and complex, the relative power located within its various structural spheres change. For example, the most powerful spheres in Europe during the early Middle Ages were the family/military and the religious realms of society (e.g., Duby, 1968, 1980; Hay, 2001; Huizinga, 1967). Individuals obtained power based more on their familial heritage or "station in life" than on their wealth. Most family domains were self-contained. There was no separate realm of society called a government, as these functions were assumed under the responsibilities of the family (i.e., the court). In addition, there was little commerce outside of small towns and villages. Each family estate was largely self-sufficient and determined its own economic rituals, regulations, and currency. As a result, those who lived outside these family estates (e.g., independent craftsmen, merchants, traders) often had less power than aristocrats. Similarly, the educational realm had little autonomous influence in feudal Europe. Prior to the printing press and the production of cheap rag paper, the distribution of knowledge was extremely limited, and children were taught by their family or the clergy, and scholarship in the early Middle Ages was confined to monasteries.

However, by the mid-twentieth century, the structural realms through which power was exerted in Europe had changed dramatically. By this time, the political, economic, and media spheres of society had become more powerful (e.g., Habermas, 1975; Merriman, 1996; Palmer, 1965). The religious and military spheres still exerted significant influence over society as a whole, but much less than during the early Middle Ages. Education, as a sphere of society that emerged with the formation of universities in the thirteenth century and then the Enlightenment, has continued to gain power during the last four centuries (Haskins, 1972 [1923]), and the family estates have receded from public power in modern European nation states. As a realm of society gains power, it increasingly becomes a site for contestation and struggle to dominate the discourse (Foucault, 1970; Gee, 1990) within it, which in turn influences the national narrative or what Foucault (1970) would call a culture's "regimes of truth."

From a reformist perspective, perhaps the most important alteration in the balance of power has been the emergence and increased power of an imperfect, democratically controlled political realm in Western cultures (e.g., Gilbert and Gilbert, 1989; Willis, 1999). It is important to remember that during the early Middle Ages, the government was predominantly a tool for the aristocracy and the church. After the Enlightenment and with the rise of liberalism, the political sphere began to represent the interests of the bourgeoisie and the emerging intellectual and intelligentsia classes. In the United States, it was not until the twentieth century that the political realm of society started to become more accessible to the interests of the urban working class and other previously marginalized and otherized groups (e.g., women, Jewish, African, Asian, Latino Americans). The emergence of a political sphere that is accessible to diverse interests, and the government's new power to directly influence and regulate (although not control) the economic sphere of society for the benefit of its citizens has been a significant struggle throughout the twentieth century.

As Habermas (1975) noted, these realms of society are deeply intertwined. Each realm of society significantly influences the others to various degrees depending upon the social phenomena in question. With this understanding, it is possible to view, for example, Leninism as the consolidation of societal power into the political realm of society. Lenin established a political system that eventually controlled all other realms (e.g., the media, education, recreation, religion, military) of the Soviet society. In functioning liberal democratic societies, the political realm has limitations on its power (e.g., freedom of speech and association, separation of church and state), but can potentially exert significant influence over the economic (e.g., work safety, minimum wage, disclosure of information, over-time laws) and other realms (e.g., education, media) of society (Zakaria, 2003). Although from a reformist perspective, the right of a democratically elected political realm to directly influence the other spheres of society is central for the promotion of social justice and economic fairness (e.g., Barber, 1998; Fraser, 1997; Gilbert and Gilbert, 1989; Rorty, 1998), it also embraces the concept that this political realm should not become all powerful. Ideally, no single sphere of society should completely dominate the others.

The structural basis for the distribution of power within the United States is fluid. It shifts and moves in and out of different realms of society that are constantly gaining and losing power relative to the other spheres at various times and over specific phenomena. Currently, schools are under mounting pressure from the political realm of society, as state and federal legislators assume greater control over the curriculum, nature of instruction, and assessment of children's learning through the establishment of official "standards" (i.e., areas of content and skill development) and high-stakes testing. As we discuss below, the political realm is, in turn, greatly influenced by the economic and religious realms of society. As educational reformers and scholars, we obviously devote most of our energies working within the educational sphere of society, but in order to adequately respond to the challenges facing teachers, administrators, students, and their families, it is necessary to understand that schools do not operate in a vacuum, but rather in a complex web of structural interconnections.

Class and Class Struggle

In addition to moving away from Marx's economic determinism, we have also taken liberties with his conceptualization of class and class struggle. As Gouldner (1979) insightfully noted, Marx's analysis of class struggle was rooted in an inaccurate economic dualism.

The history of all hitherto existing society is the history of class struggles. Freeman and slave, patrician and plebeian, lord and serf, guild-master and journeyman—in a word, oppressor and oppressed, stood in constant opposition to one another. . . . Our epoch . . . has simplified the class antagonisms . . . into two great hostile camps . . . : [the] Bourgeoisie and Proletariat. (Marx and Engles, 1977 [1848], p. 222)

However, according to Gouldner and others (e.g., Lachmann, 2000), throughout western history, the primary struggle between classes has not been between the weak and the strong (e.g., serfs against aristocracy), but between the two most powerful classes at the time (e.g., clergy vs. the aristocracy during the early Middle Ages, the bourgeoisie vs. the aristocracy at the end of the Middle Ages; the intellectuals and intelligentsia vs. bourgeoisie during modernism).

In addition, economic class interests have never been uniform. As Bernstein, Engles' protégé, noted by the turn of the last century, "The bourgeoisie is a highly complex class which is composed of a large number of strata with very divergent . . . interests" (quoted in Gay, 1979 [1952], p. 216). As will be discussed later in this chapter, several individuals within the English bourgeoisie and intellectual classes joined industrial workers in their advocacy to establish unions and collective bargaining rights, create a progressive tax system, redistribute wealth to fund government programs aimed at alleviating the cruel working conditions of early industrial capitalism, and revise capitalism in ways to produce wealthier middle and working classes (e.g., Hobson, 1900, 1920; Webb, 1901). Equally divergent interests could (and can) be found among intellectuals, intelligentsia, industrial workers, farmers, and even the aristocracy that still exists in some regions of the world.

Nor can class interest be scientifically determined as Marx originally implied. Even today, several contemporary Marxist scholars articulate what is in the "interest" of the working class (and by extension the vast majority of people in society) that is highly debatable (Gouldner, 1979). For example, ecological considerations of producing paper goods might be in the long-term interests of workers in paper mills (living with clean air and water), but against their short-term interests (losing jobs due to changes in the way paper is produced). In some cases, international trade is "good" for some and "bad" for other members of the working class. War serves the interests of some capitalists and is contradictory to the interests of other capitalists. Most importantly, people, as individuals or as members of a particular class, act upon what they perceive as their common interests, not on what can supposedly be scientifically determined as in their interest. The notion that if the working class, at a given moment, is not acting in accordance to what Marx viewed as in their interest and that they are thus victims of "false consciousness" is particularly anathema to reform leftists who question the wisdom of anyone, including intellectuals, identifying the public interests for other classes or individuals.

Most important, for the purposes of this book, is the perspective that class should be liberated from its economic roots. Rather than viewing class as emerging directly from the economic structure of a society, we have found it more useful to understand it as a form of collective identity that may emerge from either proprietary or nonproprietary public interests. While Marx argued that one's class (as a form of collective identity) was determined by his/her occupation, from a reform-leftist perspective, people have historically formed themselves into classes (i.e., collective public identities) based not only upon economic interests, but also on interests rooted in, for example, ethnic and geographical origins, religious beliefs, language, age, gender, and most recently, sexual orientation.[5] Understanding class as a manifestation of collective identity is especially relevant in nation states that have taken steps since World War II to legitimize the existence of diverse group identities.

As people who share a given collective public identity become aware of their common concerns, they form organizations (e.g., labor unions and interest groups such as the AFL-CIO, NOW, AARP, Christian Coalition, NAACP) and coalitions (e.g., political parties, political action committees) to promote their "discourse" (e.g., Foucault, 1970; Gee, 1990) and struggle over public life within any one or all of the previously discussed realms of society.

The manifestation of power is made more complex in diverse societies because individuals often are members of several (and at times competing) classes. An elderly African American, retired business woman might identify herself as belonging to any number of classes, including senior citizens, Christians, Blacks, women, and the bourgeoisie. Her ideology and public support for various policies and projects would likely depend upon this complex web of class identities (e.g., Maalouf, 2001; Pattillo-McCoy, 1999; Wolfe, 1998; Zou and Trueba, 1998, Zweigenhaft and Domhoff, 1991, 1998). As we enter the next century, there is little doubt that new classes will emerge and exert their influence on society. For example, marriages between people from different ancestral heritages is commonplace in the United States now, and these unions are producing offspring that within a few generations will no doubt result in the emergence of new collective identities. Although the bourgeoisie has remained the most powerful class in the United States during its 200-year history, the influence of other classes, such as intellectuals and intelligentsia, women, industrial workers, the elderly, Asians, African Americans, and Latinos can easily be recognized especially since the end of World War II. There is always a class within any given society that will, at any given point in history, have more power than other classes. For example, as previously indicated, in Iran the most powerful class is the clergy while in the twentieth-century Marxist experiments, the individuals with the most power were members of the intellectual and intelligentsia classes (e.g., Gouldner, 1979; Konrád and Szelenyi, 1979; Kornai, 1992). Finally, history clearly indicates that the power (or even the existence) of any given class will not automatically continue indefinitely.

Most importantly, reform leftists do not view any one class as having an inherently moral positionality over other classes. Neither the industrial working class, intellectuals, nor the bourgeoisie are intrinsically more ethical, insightful, or beneficial for a given society than any other class. Reform leftists reject the notion that a particular class is innately evil and thus entitled to be otherized. In particular, although reform leftists often are at odds with the desires of and thus struggle against the bourgeoisie, they also recognize their fundamental value to society as a whole. In particular, reform leftists often support the interests of the petty bourgeoisie while they are ever watchful and often critical of large corporations due to the influence they wield in many spheres of society (Schumacher, 1973).[6] However, we strongly agree with Marx's view that differences between classes do not reflect legitimate relations of superiority or inferiority among the individuals who, for whatever reason, find themselves in one aggregate versus another. All occupations in a given society are important and should provide those who work full time (even if unskilled), in societies that have solved the problem of scarcity, with a prosperous livelihood;[7] all people who live in a given society should have the same civil and political rights, and all individuals should be treated with respect and dignity. From a reformist perspective, no one should assume that because they have more wealth, are of a specific gender, or have a particular ancestral heritage, that they are "better" human beings than those who have less property or a different gender or heritage. As a result, reform leftists often speak out against racism, sexism, heterosexism, poverty, and other forms of human oppression.

However, because classes do not possess, at any given time, equal power within a given polity, it is crucial for leftists to understand the importance of coalition-building in struggles for social justice within various realms of society, and for the continued reform of democratic rituals and structures to broaden the participation of marginalized citizens. History teaches reformers that when classes join together to form political parties, generate social movements and campaigns, and push for and support social litigation, they have often been successful (Buechler, 2000). However, it is crucial to remember that these coalitions are not forever bound together. For example, during the past century, intellectuals and the proletariat in the United States have often worked together; however, they split over this country's pursuit of the Vietnam War (Gitlin, 1993; Isserman and Kazin, 2000; Rorty, 1998), the women's movement (e.g., Kessler-Harris, 2001; Rosen, 2001, Staggenborg, 1998), and the ecology movement (Gouldner, 1979; Gottlieb, 2005). Even today, as Bush's proposal to drill for oil in Alaska demonstrates, the proletariat and the bourgeoisie at times form a coalition against intellectuals, the intelligentsia, and women to promote economic development over ecological conservation.

Perhaps our most significant divergence from Marx's conceptualization of class analysis lies in his proposition that the abolishment of capitalism would result in the demise of classes and the end of class struggle. While on the surface Marx's notion of a classless society appears noble—even utopian—as Gouldner (1979, 1980) indicates, in reality it represents potential nightmare. Specifically, what does this universal class do with those individuals who do not, for whatever reason, identify with it? A social theory that advocates for the end of classes and class conflict is potentially treacherous in that it provides a moral justification to squelch opposition since, in the ideal society, there should be no class antagonisms. If there is only one legitimate class in society, then anyone who disagrees with those who claim to represent this all-inclusive class (and who have the power to defend this representation) can easily be otherized as outlaws, rather than people who merely have different perspectives or collective identities. The freedom for an individual to select or create his/her own collective identity, and the existence of a *public* and peaceful struggle between classes are essential aspects of a democratic society, and should, therefore, never come to an end. Now that the notion of class has been clarified for the purposes of this chapter, we turn our attention to the current right-wing coalition that has dominated the educational policy debate in the United States for the last quarter of the twentieth century.

The Conservative Coalition

The coalition behind the conservative restoration consists primarily of four traditionally powerful classes of people in our society: the bourgeoisie, the technical intelligentsia, fundamentalist Christians, and Euro-American males. On the surface, it is easy to see why this restoration has been so successful. The interests of these classes not only reflect deep historical U.S. traditions (e.g., capitalism, Christianity, individualism, science, and technology), but they also represent the two wealthiest classes in America, and thus have had ample funds to promote their agenda.

The dominant, educational discourse in the United States continues to be driven, as it has throughout most of its history, by market forces. As Apple (1996, 2001) and others (e.g., Barber, 1992; Giroux, 1999) have noted, the most powerful class within the conservative coalition (and the country, at large), the bourgeoisie, has successfully framed the educational discourse during most of the twentieth century within an economic context. Throughout western history, the goal of the bourgeoisie has been to create conditions favorable for doing business. The primary concern of this class has always been the generation and accumulation of wealth. In addition, the bourgeoisie has an individualistic orientation towards wealth entitlement. Most members of this class believe that they are entitled to the wealth they acquire during their lives, and all attempts to redistribute this wealth is a form of oppression. This stance is often justified in their belief in a meritocracy. Rather than viewing their accumulation of wealth as the result of a complex web of arbitrary and contingent circumstances,[8] they believe it is due to their individual or familial efforts and talents. For example, as we have discussed elsewhere, during the first half of the twentieth century, members of the bourgeoisie argued that their place of power and privilege in society was an example of Darwin's theory of evolution (Goodman, 1992). These individuals argued that their power and wealth indicated their natural superiority over others, and thus represented an evolution of the species (a concept known as Social Darwinism). By having the strongest (best businessmen) dominate over the "less-worthy" members of society, the species as a whole will more likely evolve towards perfection.

As one might suspect, since the advent of public schooling in the United States, the bourgeoisie have argued that schools should operate as a business. Rather than build more school houses, as public education spread, their architecture and operations resembled those found in industrial factories rather than homes. Rather than focusing most of our attention on the welfare and unique talents of children as individuals and members of a community, the bourgeoisie consistently advocated that our primary concern be with the *products* of education (e.g., technical skills, academic content), efficiency of operations, and accountability that the money spent on the education of children is not wasted. The results of this influence can easily be witnessed by spending just a few hours in most public classrooms (e.g., Apple, 1986; Duffy et al., 1987; Goodman, 1988). In response, during the last three decades, many school districts have adopted prepackaged instructional programs as the basis for the classroom curriculum. These programs are specifically designed to raise pupils' scores on state and/or national standardized tests, and they come complete with specified objectives (i.e., content), step-by-step instructional procedures (dominated by workbooks and drills), and quantitative exams to measure exactly what pupils learn. Instead of establishing relevant and meaningful curricular goals, identifying intellectually stimulating topics of study, and designing thoughtful learning experiences based on an intimate knowledge of their own and their pupils' interests and talents, teachers have been relegated to a managerial rather than educative role. In the vast majority of schools, teachers' work resembles that of shop floor managers who coordinate the day's work (schedule time for each subject, organize children into ability groups, assign seat work, maintain paperwork on students' completed assignments, administer programmatic tests, and discipline pupils to keep them on task when necessary), rather than intellectually engaging children about the world in which they live and will inherit. Getting the children through these programs on time in a smooth, quiet, and orderly fashion has become the main criterion upon which teachers are evaluated. As Zeichner (1986, p. 88) noted more than fifteen years ago,

> [N]umerous analyses, conducted from a variety of ideological and political perspectives, have concluded that the effect of many of the recent policies

affecting teachers has been to promote greater external control over the content, processes, and outcomes of teachers' work and to encourage teachers to adopt conformist orientations to self and society as well as technical orientations to the role of teacher.

One does not need to be a scholar of labor studies to see that schools have, during the last century, adopted an industrial organizational structure found in corporate business. From this perspective, principals are building executives, responsible for the physical plant and staff; teachers are shop floor managers who oversee the activities of students; and students are assembly-line workers who must keep up with the work schedule. Under recent legislation passed by the Bush administration, scores on standardized, high-stakes tests are now the school's "product." If a school cannot produce this product in a cost effective manner, then it is threatened with sanctions just as an inefficiently run business suffers consequences when it doesn't perform.

As Solo's (2000) analysis of several economies during the twentieth century indicates, wealth is most successfully created as a result of the symbiotic relationship between markets (which produce funds for research and marketing) and technological development (i.e., the application of scientific information for improving the everyday material condition of humans). For example, the last two decades have been similar to what transpired during the 1920s with the electrification of the country, the development of the telephone, and the expanded use of automobiles and trucks (e.g., Ling, 1992; Nye, 1990; Potter, 1974). Technological advancements in communications and transportation have significantly altered the type, quantity, and manner in which products and services are produced, delivered, and consumed in the United States. Just as electrical production required workers to obtain more education and skills, the products and services being developed within this technologically advanced environment require significantly more education than was the case with older types of industrial production.

As a result, members of the bourgeoisie have advocated for specifically defining and raising academic skills (e.g., written and oral expression, reading comprehension, basic reasoning and logic, ability to locate and compile information, math computation) prior to graduating high school and for greater accountability (through standardized testing) to ensure these graduates can perform these utilitarian tasks (e.g., Allington, 2002). Although their calls for improved education are now situated in a universal context such as President Bush's "No Child Left Behind" legislation, given the conservative policy recommendations and lack of funding for improving public schools, their concerns are rarely geared towards those children who are most marginalized in our society. (After all, their primary concern is with having a significant number of workers, rather than the population as a whole, who are educated to be members of the technical intelligentsia.) Having a pool of poorly educated individuals in society is not particularly worrisome to this class, given the need for low-skilled, poorly paid service jobs that also make the U.S. economy work.

This agenda, they claim, is necessary in order to maintain our country's prosperity in light of the increasingly interconnected and competitive global market place. Young people who do not have access to quality education, a history of well-educated family members, or wealth to pay for tutors, as well as those who are not academically inclined or talented, or who do not have command of the current dialect of power (i.e., TV English) suffer greatly as a result of the sorting that takes place due to this accountability agenda (Spring, 1989). In addition, many individuals within the bourgeoisie have traditionally viewed government involvement in people's lives, such as the education of children and other government-sponsored programs and policies (e.g., economic opportunities for marginalized classes, progressive tax system), as antithetical to individual freedom and liberty, and thus have championed calls to minimize public support for those children who lack access to quality schools and support calls to fund education through vouchers; thus privatizing the schooling of children.[9]

Another powerful class in the conservative coalition is the intelligentsia. As Gouldner (1979) notes, this class is made up of people who have obtained a post-secondary education and utilize the current cultural capital in performance of their occupations. Many of these occupations are in the relatively well-paid service sector of the economy such as lawyers, doctors, teachers, nurses, accountants, therapists, politicians, government bureaucrats, and clergy. Of course, many members of the intelligentsia work in industry. Today, nearly all managers, sales personnel, and technicians who work in business are members of the intelligentsia rather than the industrial "working class" (individuals without post-high-school education and who work primarily with their hands in the manufacturing of products). In fact, as Galbraith (1987) and Gouldner (1979) note, even the top managers of corporations are often members of the intelligentsia rather than the bourgeoisie class. In fact, with the exception of the petty bourgeoisie, this class, which was so public in the nineteenth century (Himmelberg, 1994), is difficult to identify in today's corporate structure (Garten, 2001). Rarely is there a single individual who owns and runs his/her own large corporation. Today, most CEOs are employees of a corporation who are professionally educated and trained for these responsibilities. They are hired and fired by a board of directors who own significant amounts of stock in the corporation. One could argue that the greatest beneficiaries of the conservative restoration has been the intelligentsia. This is perhaps obvious in an economy based, not upon muscle power or the amount of land one owns, but rather upon the ability to acquire and utilize knowledge. An economy that is based (especially its growth) upon scientific and technological developments will naturally reward those who are talented in these domains. For example, the significant rise in income inequality that began in the 1970s and has continued until today (with a brief closing of the gap during the Clinton administration) is due primarily to the increased wages given to members of the intelligentsia who work in corporate culture. Since the emergence of the "post-industrial" service economy in the United States (Bell, 1973), there has been an increased demand for individuals who have obtained and who can utilize the current and evolving cultural capital. As a result, many (especially young adults) within intelligentsia have been strongly supportive of the previously mentioned conservative economic, political, and most importantly, educational policies, and their membership in the conservative coalition has been central to its exercise of power.

The third class in this coalition is composed of various sects of fundamentalist Christians in our society, or what some refer to as the "Christian Right." Although the most recent class to join the conservative coalition, they represent its most ardent, grassroots activists. Unlike the bourgeoisie or the intelligentsia, the public interests of this class are not primarily economic. At a time when other religious fundamentalists around the world are attacking the United States as a symbol of decadent excess, the Christian Right in this country has accepted much of what modernism has to offer a society, namely, its consumerism and prosperity. However, they are highly critical of what they view as the "crassness" of modern society. Their concerns are focused chiefly upon what they perceive as the moral degradation of the United States due to the influence of secularism, humanism, feminism, homosexuality, science, immigration, and unfettered access to a wide range of information (especially anything associated with sex outside of heterosexual marriage). They want a nation (and one suspects the world) based upon a fundamentalist interpretation of Western, Judeo-Christian traditions (Hunter, 1991). As Buchanan (2002) demonstrates, this class is particularly concerned about the undermining of the Euro-American identity as the standard of what it means to be a citizen of this country and institutions which they argue should be based solely upon this particular ancestral heritage. If government is to play a role in the lives of its citizens, it should be used to promote these traditions, and to discourage the legitimation of contrary narratives, images, rituals, myths, values, and/or beliefs.

Within the educational realm of society, this class strongly supports an agenda to control the scientific and social content of our children's curriculum. For example, they have proposed (and in a few places successfully passed) laws that would either bar the teaching of evolution or present "creation science" or "intelligent design" as a theory of equal validity (e.g., Binder, 2002; Fraser, 1999). This class has also been deeply involved in struggles over what is taught in our history courses given the importance this subject has in forming our collective national identity (e.g., Nash et al., 1997; Symcox, 2002; Zimmerman, 2002). They are especially concerned about "multicultural education" in which children are encouraged to respect and even celebrate the diverse ancestral heritages of our people (Sleeter and Grant, 1999) and bilingual education (Crawford, 1991, 2000) which they see as a direct threat to children who should assimilate the dominant, northern European cultural influence on our society. They have been vocal supporters of the previously mentioned "skills-based" curriculum due to their desire to keep what they perceive as "humanistic values" from being taught in public schools. Their support for vouchers is rooted in their desire to have their tax dollars support religious schools, which they believe are more likely to teach "American" (i.e., conservative) ideas and values (Doerr, 1996).

The final class within this coalition is made up of people that many fail to see as a class with particular public interests. This class consists of males who identify themselves with the Euro-American heritage in the United States. This class has felt "under attack" throughout most of the second half of the twentieth century. The gains in political, social, and economic power of women and people of color during the last five decades has often been viewed by many Euro-American males as "at their expense" (Zou and Trueba, 1998). Prior to this time period, the privileges enjoyed by Euro-American males were taken for granted by nearly everyone. Although still dominant, it was not too long ago that this class had exclusive access to the most powerful realms of society, namely, business, government, and the media (Zweigenhaft and Domhoff, 1991, 1998). As a result, they resent the access that other classes have won to these societal spheres. They are particularly threatened by efforts to alter the traditional identity of what it means to be an American, which has historically been based upon mythic images of individuals like George Washington, Thomas Jefferson, and Alexander Hamilton. As one of their most outspoken advocates notes (Buchanan, 2002), until recently, all immigrants who came to the United States were strongly encouraged to assimilate themselves into this Euro-American tradition and identity. To become American, from this perspective, is to adopt (as much as possible) the appearance, characteristics, values, traditions, ideals, knowledge, and mannerisms associated with having an ancestral heritage rooted in the male dominated history of northwestern Europe. Those who had difficulty doing so, such as people of color or women, were simply expected to "get by" the best they could.

Similar to evangelical Christians, this class is primarily interested in the content of our children's social curriculum. They fear the evolution of an American identity that reflects the authentic cultural and gender diversity of its citizenry (Lynch, 2002). To this class, notions of an America that has incorporated and benefitted greatly from the ways in which this nation is Native American, Asian, African, Latin, and female (except as supporters of their men) is anathema to their conception of what has made this country "great." They desire a curriculum that encourages children from various ancestral heritages (and genders) to recognize the unique and overwhelmingly valuable contribution to this country that has come directly from the patriarchal, Anglo-Saxon Protestant tradition in Europe (e.g., our Founding Fathers).

One does not have to be a sociologist to recognize the power of these classes in our society. Their public interests have extremely deep roots in the history of the United States. Capitalism, Christianity, patriarchy, European Puritanism, individualism, and a suspicion of government have, among large numbers of our population, been sacrosanct in the United States. Given the make-up of this coalition and the similarity of their values to the deeply rooted, dominant heritage of America, we should not be surprised at the success of their agenda. The power of this coalition makes working for the progressive education of our nation's children more difficult than perhaps at most other times in our history. However, the idea that this coalition is "all powerful" is a myth we should strongly contest.

Unfortunately, many leftist academics fail to see that there is a coalition of classes that oppose much of the conservative resurgence (e.g., Apple, 2001; Giroux, 1999; McLaren, 2000). This coalition is composed of many intellectuals (e.g., professors, scholars, artists) who, in the West, have a long history of advocating for the "universal good" and for public decisions to be made based upon the intelligent generation and deliberation of information; many individuals within the intelligentsia (particularly lawyers, political activists, journalists, educators, nurses, entertainers) who believe power and influence should rest in the hands of those who utilize academic and artistic knowledge in everyday life; unionized industrial and low-wage workers who want decisions based upon employment security and job opportunities; the majority of African, Jewish, non-Cuban Latino, Asian American, and women who have over the last several decades seen the benefits that come from a society that legitimates and honors the cultural diversity and peoples of our population; and even a few members of the bourgeoisie (e.g., Soros, 2002) who recognize that it is in their long term, economic self-interest to have a more democratic and socially just society.

While opposing much of the conservative agenda, this coalition is considerably weaker due, in part, to its lack of relative wealth and ardor. Unfortunately, many within this opposing coalition have failed to resist significant parts of the conservative educational agenda. For example, many members of these classes are supportive of efforts to define and raise academic standards since they recognize the material and political benefits that can be found in societies with a well-educated work force and citizenry, and have only just begun to question the use of high-stakes testing and standards as the best way to improve the education of our children. Adding to their support for the conservative educational agenda is the failure of leftist educators to articulate and/or obtain a public forum in which to express a compelling, alternative vision of schooling based upon a noneconomic (e.g., democratic, existential) rationale.[10]

As school reformers, we work primarily with members of the intelligentsia (e.g., teachers, administrators, school support staff). Unfortunately, these members of the intelligentsia are not particularly powerful. First, the educational sphere (in which we all work) is not nearly as powerful as the political, economic, or media realms of society. Second, many of these individuals do not have a long history of being members of the intelligentsia. In most cases, the parents of the teachers and administrators with whom we work were (are) members of the working class. In addition, due to the fact that the education of children is viewed as "women's work," educators are not afforded the same respect and stature as members of the intelligentsia who work in industry or government (Apple, 1986). Third, we also work closely with two classes of people who have virtually no power in our society, namely, poor children and their parents. Although we have worked with and tried to influence the thinking of politicians, business people, and those in the media, the resources we have to do this type of work has been extremely limited. Given the lack of power these classes have relative to the other classes mentioned in this chapter, some may ask, "why bother?" However, it would be a mistake to assume that alterations in a complex society must flow from the top down. To the contrary, it has been our experience (as discussed in chapters 3–6) that, while difficult, much can be accomplished at the "grassroots" level.

CONCLUSION: REFLECTIONS ON CHAPTER 1

This chapter has examined the socio-political context in which progressive educators are currently working. It is not a particularly supportive environment. The public discourse on education and recent government policies such as the No Child Left Behind Act can undermine our spirits and encourage us to retreat into our private thoughts. However, it is crucial that we do not become overly discouraged. As we look throughout history, we find it filled with dark times only to be followed by new breakthroughs and progressive leaps. In spite of the conservative nature of our society, there are many educators who are not giving up, and who are determined to provide more meaningful and socially responsible schooling for our children. These individuals are resolved to collaborate, and through this collaboration, deepen the education of their students in spite of the current atmosphere of mistrust and fear that has been generated by the previously discussed conservative coalition of classes in our country.

As will be discussed in the next chapter, our own efforts to foster the education of children based upon values of democracy, social justice, and existential meaning have taken place primarily among those who actually work in school buildings (e.g., teachers, administrators, parents, students, support staff). Although we have, on occasion, entered into both the political and public spheres of society (e.g., speaking at legislative committee hearings, lobbying for legislation, organizing public forums, writing for professional and public magazines), our paramount efforts have been focused on the occupational discourse that occurs among those who work in and send their children to schools.[11]

This book represents an attempt to portray our work, and in light of this portrayal, raise several issues that have emerged as a result of our efforts. The purpose of this book is to contribute to the current progressive, educational discourse on school reform that is occurring throughout the United States in spite of conservative efforts to denounce and misrepresent its historical and current efforts (e.g., Ravitch, 2000). Toward this goal, in the next chapter, we explore the origins and ideological foundation of the Harmony Education Center and describe the steps we took in generating the topics discussed within this book. Chapters 3 and 4 illuminate our efforts to alter the culture of several individual schools in an attempt to make them more democratic and, once established, use these democratic rituals, values, and governance structure to stimulate progressive curricular and pedagogical reforms. Chapter 5 examines the substance of the deliberations that emerged from our work with the previously mentioned schools in the context of the current conservative educational agenda. The final chapter provides a commentary on our ongoing struggles to work toward the progressive reforming of schools in an increasingly conservative United States.

CHAPTER 2

Creating a Progressive Educational Organization: Harmony Education Center in Its Historical Context

The Harmony Education Center came into existence in 1990 as a result of a partnership that was formed between Harmony School and Indiana University. In this section, we briefly recount the origins of this center and provide an account of the historical tradition within which we place our work. This placement is useful in establishing a context in which to situate our current efforts to make education more democratic and existentially meaningful to those who work in our schools. Finally, we will discuss the details regarding the analysis of our efforts that served as the basis for this book.

ORIGINS AND IDEOLOGICAL ORIENTATION

Approximately, fifteen years ago, the author of this book conducted field work for an interpretive study of Harmony School, an independent, pre-K–12 grade school based upon a democratic ethos and located in Bloomington, Indiana (Goodman, 1992). A few years after the field work was completed, the Harmony Education Center (HEC) was established for the purpose of fostering conversations between the educators at Harmony and other reform-minded educators, policy makers, and scholars. During the last decade, our understanding of this work and the society in which we live has continuously evolved. In broad terms, the ultimate purpose of Harmony Education Center is to support and engage those who work in schools and who are interested in creating educational experiences and environments that will help foster the movement of society towards the creation of a more liberal, social, and critical democracy. The term *critical* is used in the sense that it is unwise to take a given notion of democracy for granted (as many

*Thanks to Daniel Baron and Steve Bonchek for their assistance with this chapter.

people do in our society). In a critical democracy, the meaning of democracy, itself, is always contested. In addition, every institution and organization, proposed and/or implemented policy, political party, public individual, law, ritual, social value, and history is vulnerable and open to public critique. As previously mentioned, in a critical democracy class struggle is "in the open." Within such a polity, there is tolerance for a wide range of public commentary and action as long as it remains nonviolent. As scholars and reformers, this commitment to open critique is central to our occupational endeavors. Ever since the scholastic tradition emerged within western universities during the Middle Ages (Baldwin, 1997), public critique has been a significant component of academic and journalistic discourses within functioning democracies.

As most social scholars recognize, the adjective "liberal" comes from the tradition of liberalism that swept Europe, and its descendant states such as the United States, between the seventeenth and twentieth centuries. Although we reject the excessive individualism embedded in traditional European liberalism that has been so dominant throughout the history of the United States, its value as a social ideology should not be completely discounted in efforts to deepen our democracy through the education of our children (e.g., Bellah et al., 1985; Damico, 1978; Dewey, 1930; Huber, 1971; Lasch, 1978; Lukes, 1973; Nisbet, 1990; Peck, 1987; Sennett, 1977; Wood, 1972). Liberalism's historical value continues to lie in the attention it gives to basic rights and liberties that all individuals should have in a democratic society. Individuals must be not only free but also supported in their efforts to "self-actualize" (Fromm, 1956; Maslow, 1976). The ability and freedom to focus on one's desires, fears, hopes, dreams, and creativity in order to existentially "know oneself," is crucial for any society that wishes to promote human dignity. A liberal democracy also provides numerous opportunities for individuals to lead, as much as possible, self-determined lives. Individuals in a functioning, democratic society have the liberty to pursue their inner callings, to achieve beyond typical expectations, and to have those achievements recognized and rewarded. Most importantly, our conception of democracy is deeply rooted in the notion that society is actively tolerant of individual uniqueness and self-expression regarding such matters as religion, ethnic heritage, race, gender, sexual preference, emerging lifestyles, social and political ideas, and the creative and performing arts. In short, human diversity is celebrated and embraced as a social value.

Finally, our reference to the word "social" comes from Dewey's (1946 [1929]) conception of social pragmatism. As Dewey (1927) argued, although democracy's primary function is to resolve class (and other types of) conflict without resorting to violence in a given society, it can also be viewed as a way of life rather than merely a set of societal rituals (e.g., voting) and governmental structures (e.g., congress, president):

A democracy is more than a form of government; it is primarily a mode of associated living, of conjoint communicated experience. The extension in space of the number of individuals who participate in an interest so that each has to refer his own action to that of others, and to consider the action of others to give point and direction to his [or her] own, is equivalent to the breaking down of those barriers of class, race, and national territory which kept men from perceiving the full import of their activity. (Dewey, 1966 [1916], p. 87)

This latter notion of democracy is particularly important since, as will be discussed later, the primary focus of the Harmony Education Center is to bring collaborative values, structures, and habits of interaction to schools and other educational communities for the purpose of educating children to find personal meaning within the context of a democratic community.

From Dewey's perspective, democratic living calls upon us to recognize our connection to others both inside and outside the particular polity within which we live, and calls upon our voluntary commitment to their general welfare. In this light, several scholars have called for a greater understanding of what Fraser (1997) calls the "politics of recognition," that is, the connection between identity and social justice. Of particular importance is the dynamic of what Rorty (1989) refers to as our "we" consciousness. As previously mentioned in our discussion of class consciousness, in addition to having an individual identity, Rorty notes that we also have any number of collective identities rooted in our families, our ancestral heritages, our gender, our age, the color of our skin, and our occupation, among other things. Typically, a given individual will feel a greater connection to other people who share one or more of their collective identities than to those who do not. As a result, this individual is more likely to care about the welfare of these fellow compatriots. Rorty (1998) and others (e.g., Barber, 1998; Bodnar, 1996; Nussbaum, 1996; Viroli, 1995) have recently advocated for the development of a collective identity based upon our national polity *to the degree that this collective identity acknowledges our diversity as a people (e.g., ancestral, gender, sexual orientation, physical or mental abilities) and is committed to the politics of inclusion and social justice.* That is, they argue for a nationalism based, not upon a particular ancestral heritage, but upon a mutually recognized (although imperfect and contested) social contract, or what Habermas (1994) refers to as "constitutional patriotism." For example, Rorty calls for the left within the United States to justify their advocacy for equality, opportunity, inclusion, respect, and caregiving, not upon a particular economic class or system, but upon our national identity. If this identity took hold firmly among the electorate, then as Americans, "we" simply would not allow 20 percent of our children to live in poverty or to attend grossly inadequate schools, for a significant number of our society to go without basic medical care, or for citizens be marginalized or otherized based upon skin color, ethnicity, body type, gender, or sexual preference (because these differences pale compared to our bonds of nationhood).

Unfortunately, many in the United States view their "we" in much more limited terms than suggested here. For example, the "we" consciousness among most individuals within the bourgeoisie and many within the intelligentsia stops at their immediate or extended family members. For the most part, patriotism and national identity are called upon only when there are external threats such as those from Al-Qaeda rather than as a rationale to promote equality and social justice. Nevertheless, Rorty notes the potential power that this national identity could have as a catalyst for bridging our "otherness." This national "we" would ideally create a foundation for members of different classes to embrace one another as "us," rather than "them." In this way, classes can engage in struggle, but this conflict is modified by our union, which is based upon geography and the imperfect social contract under which we agree to live.

Of special concern for the left is the redistribution of wealth, power, and other benefits that occur within a given society. As previously mentioned, the social contract that is the basis of a given polity is never generated by classes of equal power. As a result, all social contracts benefit some classes (elites) over others. In capitalist societies where the common denominator of power is wealth, the bourgeoisie and others (e.g., intelligentsia) with access to wealth form this elite. In twentieth-century Marxist/Leninist states, the elite was almost exclusively comprised of members of the intellectual and intelligentsia classes. The rewards that go to some classes are always disproportionate vis-à-vis other classes (Sen, 1992). As discussed in the first chapter, there will always be personal characteristics, structures, and systems of power that benefit some and not other members of that society. Since the former's "success" is contingent, in part, upon these characteristics, structures, and systems of power, it is only socially just to have a portion of this wealth, power, and benefits redistributed for the purpose of creating opportunities and protecting basic necessities and rights for those individuals who, for whatever reason, have a difficult time being successful under these same values, characteristics, structures, and/or systems (Rawls, 2001). Recognition of our collective identity as the building block for promoting social justice was central to what Dewey (1927) called the "great community."

Organizational Structure

Similar to Dewey, the Harmony Education Center views the education of children as a crucial site for the building of a more liberal, social, and critical democracy. Along with religion, popular culture, news, government and economic systems, friends, and family; schools influence the ways in which children will come to view themselves, other people, the nation state in which they live, and the world at large. In return, the children of today will influence the type of society their children will inherit, creating an endless feedback loop (Dewey, 1920).

We view educational reform as largely a matter of engaging in a variety of discourses in a diversity of settings (Gee, 1990). As a center, we seek to initiate and/or participate in conversations among democratically reform-minded scholars (e.g., university seminars, journals, books, conferences), school practitioners (e.g., administrators, teachers, staff, parents, children), educational change agents (e.g., Coalition of Essential Schools, ATLAS, Institute for Democracy and Education, Fairtest, League of Professional Schools), and philanthropic institutions (e.g., the Bay Foundation, the Philanthropic Initiative, the Lucent Foundation, Lilly Endowment). During the time of this work and up until recently, HEC consisted of three integrated components:[1]

Harmony School (HS) is an early-childhood–12th-grade school committed to democratic education, and serves as a demonstration site for school visits/debriefing sessions. Harmony teachers and students also get involved in the reform efforts of interested schools (e.g., establishing ongoing faculty seminars, demonstrating lessons and democratic classroom meetings, arranging student exchange visits and projects, participation in national educational reform meetings). Recently, Harmony School was selected as one of eleven "First Amendment" schools in the country by the Association of Curriculum and Supervision in their effort to promote the freedoms of this amendment to children. Teachers and students from each designated school met during the summer of 2002 for their first seminar and planning session. In 2004, it was selected to be one of eleven "mentor schools" in the nation by the *Coalition of Essential Schools*. Although its democratic ethos, governance structure, curriculum, and pedagogy of the school has deepened since the publication of the previously mentioned interpretive study, the study still provides a basic understanding of the educational experience found within its walls (Goodman, 1992).

The *Office for Outreach Services* (OOS), which is the main focus of this book, provides a wide range of assistance to educators engaged in substantive reform projects. Examples of the office's activities during 12 of the last 14 years include: 1) Providing leadership and facilitation of school-wide reform projects. These projects involved the entire school community in an effort to substantively alter the ways in which the school was governed, and its relationship to the community and parents. In addition, there were significant efforts made to deepen the curriculum, pedagogy, and learning experiences of the students. And facilitating 2) staff development activities on topics of progressive, democratic education; organizing meetings and conferences on topics of school reform; and collaborating with organizations that share our pedagogical and social ethos (e.g., Bay Area Coalition for Equitable Schools, Boston Center for Collaborative Education, John Dewey Center for Democracy).

The *Institute for Research* is responsible for contributions to educational scholarship, supports the inquiry work of young scholars and Harmony teachers, and provides resources (e.g., books, articles, films, speakers) to educators working with the HEC. Scholarship supported by the institute includes both collaborative and individual projects. Some of these projects include additional research into the lived experiences of Harmony School (e.g., Bintz, 1995; Goodman, 1991; Heilman and Goodman, 1996; Kuzmic, 1990; Skulnick, 2004), teacher/scholar research (e.g., Goodman, Baron, Belcher, Hastings-Hines, 1994), reports on the ways in which the school has served as a catalyst for pedagogical changes in public schools in which the Office for Outreach Services (OOS) has worked (e.g., Goodman and Kuzmic, 1997), and self-reflective analyses of the OOS such as reported in this book. In addition, the institute has supported several historical studies of education and progressive politics in the West (e.g., Goodman and Holloway, 2000).

Although each component of the center has autonomy to conduct its work in the ways it sees most beneficial to its clients and colleagues (e.g., scholars, children, educators, parents, scholars), the Budget Committee (composed of two of the center's directors, one member of the support staff, and 4 of Harmony School's teachers) oversees all financial decisions, and the Solidarity Committee (composed of one of the center's executive director [currently Steve Bonchek], one member of the support staff, and five teachers from Harmony School), which oversees and coordinates the activities of each of the previously mentioned components. Each of these components also works collaboratively. For example, teachers and students have been involved in numerous school-reform projects. Educational change agents who work for the OOS and the institute also participate in school functions, and as previously indicated, teachers and change agents help generate scholarship supported by the institute. The goal is to create an organization in which there is a rich cross pollination of ideas emerging from both contemporary and historical scholarship in a wide diversity of fields as well as from lived experiences working with educators and children.

HEC's School Reform Projects 1990–2002

Shortly after the creation of HEC, we came to the conclusion that intensive partnerships with individual schools offer great potential for fostering substantive educational reform, and as a result, for 12 years we prioritized this type of work. Given our ideological orientation, we focused many of our resources to assist several "high poverty" schools. Fortunately, our orientation coincided with the U.S. Department of Education's "Schoolwide Reform" initiative, which provided funds to schools and school districts that wanted to participate in the type of intensive partnerships we had come to value.

In our initial meetings with schools, we presented ourselves as assuming two primary roles. First, we undertook the role as constructivist/transformational leaders for the purpose of facilitating the reform process (e.g., Anderson, 1990, 1998; Blase and Anderson, 1995; Quantz, Rogers, and Dantley, 1991). Toward this goal, we typically began our work with a given school by conducting introductory interviews with the faculty, administrators, 20–30 parents, and up to one hundred or more students in small groups and whole classes (Spradley, 1979). Interview questions were modified according to the particular school, but generally included:

1. Does your school have a guiding philosophy and if so what is it? If not, what do you think should be its guiding philosophy?
2. What, in a positive sense, makes your school special?
3. What are some of the obstacles your school deals with on a regular basis?
4. If you had a magic wand that could change anything in your school, what would it be?
5. In what ways, if at all, does your school help prepare young people to live in a democratic society?

The purpose of these interviews was to elicit "stories," that in turn, illuminated the nature of a given school's culture. Based upon these data, plus information that emerged from several structured conversations with the faculty on a variety of topics (e.g., rationale for educational reform; nature and difficulties of organizational change; purposes of education; perceptions of children and their families, issues of student, teacher, and school assessment; concepts of intelligence and learning styles; relationship between schools and society), the faculty generated a vision that portrayed the ideal school they wanted to create. During the next 6–18 months (depending upon the specific situation), the school community was organized into study groups that explored areas of concern related to their vision. Based upon this study, the school community generated a plan (e.g., goals and strategies) to make their vision a reality. During the next 1–4 years (at the discretion of each school), we helped the school community implement their plan, reflect upon these efforts, and in light of this reflection, affirm or alter their strategies, goals, and/or the original vision.

The idea for this book began in 1998 when we received a grant to conduct a self study of our work as external change agents. Toward this end, we reviewed field records based upon our work with more than fifty schools in the United States from 1990–2002. From June, 1998 until June, 1999 we kept extensive field notes of our planning sessions, our intensive partnerships with five "high poverty" elementary schools, and our subsequent debriefing sessions. Finally, two graduate assistants interviewed approximately 75 percent of the faculty in these previously mentioned schools at the conclusion of or at least one year after their planning year was initiated.

This book represents the results of our reflections and deliberations. Specifically, we kept field notes on what topics and comments were expressed at each meeting within each of these five schools, on individuals' reactions (including our own) to these projects as they unfolded over time (e.g., enthusiastic, alienated, apathetic) and what individuals did in light of their reactions, and on comments expressed during follow-up interviews. The purpose of this self study was to identify what we were attempting to accomplish at these schools in light of the actual events with the people involved, rather than official statements found in brochures.

From 1998 to 2002, conversation, interview, and observation notes were reviewed regularly. Incidents and bits of information were at first coded into tentative conceptual categories. As these categories emerged, questions arose that were used to guide further investigation. The findings from subsequent observations and conversations were then compared to the initial categories. Through this "constant comparison" of data (Glaser and Strauss, 1975), the analytical themes explored in this book crystallized. As the process continued, special attention was given to data that seemed to challenge original conceptualizations (Erickson, 1986). This return to the data source, followed by modification or generation of ideas, continued until the findings could be presented in some detail. It is important to emphasize that we are not attempting to present our work as a "model" for others to follow. Rather, our goal is to portray our work and say something worthwhile about educational reform in ways that others will find meaningful.

Placing Harmony in a Socio-Historical Context: The Left, Reformist Tradition

As previously mentioned, we did not view our work in isolation. Not only do we see our work as part of a broader effort by many people and organizations to make our society more socially just, democratic, inclusive, and respectful of individual diversity and freedom, we also view it as continuing an important, but often overlooked tradition by today's leftist intellectuals and intelligentsia in the West. Although as educational change agents we look towards the future in light of present circumstances, our comprehension of these circumstances and the orientation of our work is crucially informed by our understanding of history. As Hegel (1942 [1821], pp. 12–13) stated long ago,

> Philosophy in any case always comes on the scene too late. . . . As the thought of the world, it appears only when actuality is already there cut and dried after its process of formation has been completed. . . . [H]istory's inescapable lesson, is that it is only when actuality is mature that the ideal . . .

apprehends the real world in its substance. . . . The owl of Minerva [wisdom] spreads its wings [works] only with the falling of the dusk [only after the day has past].

It is extremely difficult to understand how to conduct one's work in education or other realms of society without an understanding of history. With the passage of time, we can gain insight into what forces and events contribute to the history of a given place or people that is extremely difficult to grasp during the present. Contemporary western societies and international relationships are inordinately complex and difficult to discern. Of course, placing one's work within a historical perspective is at some level always arbitrary. There is no one history of a people, nation, region, or culture. Every history represents some form of what Williams (1977) referred to as the "selective tradition" in which events and ideas are chosen as important in light of one's orientation to human life and society. Nevertheless, one would not be able to fully grasp our work without a review of our historical understandings and the ways in which this knowledge of history influences our work as educational change agents.

We begin our discussion with a caveat. Unlike both Marx and Hegel, pragmatic reformists do not believe history has a teleology. There is no "ultimate purpose" of human beings on this planet. History is not unfolding in a rational manner toward the reconciliation of God and humankind as many religions claim, or between humankind and some grand metaphysical intelligence as Hegel implied, or between classes of people as Marx proposed. There is no preordained direction to history. At particular times and in specific places, historical events seem to move in a humane, and at other times and places in an inhumane direction. As previously mentioned, this direction often depends upon one's perspective. In the future, human societies might become more democratic, socially just, inclusive, and prosperous, or the opposite. In addition, it is impossible to trace the origins of most ideas. History is like a never-ending river. One can always go "up stream" a little further. However, for the purposes of this book, we focus on a decidedly important time in Europe, and in particular, England at the end of the nineteenth century.

The reformist left emerged as an offshoot to classical European liberalism and socialism. Classical liberalism arose in response to feudalism, aristocratic politics, and papal power (e.g., Holton, 1985; Huizinga, 1967; Lachmann, 2000; Merriman, 1996; Palmer, 1965). It grew significantly as a result of several events including the enlightenment and the rise of the intellectual and intelligentsia classes, the development of capitalism and the ascent of the merchant class, the Henrician and Protestant reformations, and the emergence of nation states. Specific events such as the Glorious Revolution of 1688 in England, the American Revolutionary War of 1776, and the French Revolution some thirteen years later served to entrench liberalism in the West. However, by the end of the nineteenth century, a rupture occurred within European and especially English liberalism, and reviewing this schism is necessary to understand the origins of the reform-leftist project.

To fully understand this split, it is necessary to review the status of the bourgeoisie and capitalism prior to the hegemony of liberalism (e.g., Holton, 1985; Huizinga, 1967; Lachmann, 2000; Merriman, 1996; Palmer, 1965). The bourgeoisie remained, for the most part, a disparaged class throughout the middle ages. These "middlers" (or middle class as they were called due to their position in society which fell between the aristocracy and the peasants) were denigrated due to their interest in making money, which was considered below or unworthy the aspirations of "true" gentlemen (the aristocracy), theologians/clergy, and serfs/peasants (who had the noble task of working the land).[2] Of particular consternation for the bourgeoisie were laws that singled them out as the sole source for taxation. Those merchants who managed to obtain significant wealth sought to escape this stigma and tax by purchasing "titles," building lavish homes in the countryside, and in every way possible mimicking the values, styles, and customs of the aristocracy.

By the start of the nineteenth century, a more "modern" bourgeoisie (and their supporters from the growing class of intellectuals such as Adam Smith, Jeremy Bentham, and David Ricardo) overtly challenged and rejected the path taken by wealthy merchants of the previous centuries. These modern bourgeoisie (often referred to as the Manchester Men, given the central role that city played in the development of industrial capitalism) and intellectuals were determined to defeat the remaining aspects of feudalism in which one's place in society (i.e., serfs, guild members, aristocracy, priests, or merchants) and the power, privileges, benefits, and social status that come with one's caste was determined by family heritage. They argued that society should be a meritocracy. One's place in society should be based solely on an individual's talents, hard work, and good fortune. Everyone should have a chance to pursue his interests and become successful (women were not generally viewed as having a rightful place in public life at this time). No one should be rewarded or limited merely because of their family heritage or religion; no one should exercise power based upon "divine intervention;" and no one should be considered above the rule of law. Everyone, including the aristocracy, should work for the wealth they obtained, and all men should have inalienable rights such as freedom of speech, association, and religion; democracy; and ownership of property.

In addition, they fiercely sought to eradicate the contempt for a life of money making. As Weber (1998 [1946]) noted in his classic study, seeking profit was promoted as morally righteous (i.e., encouraged the values of hard work, ambition, persistence, saving/investment, and self-reliance). After all, within two hundred years, capitalism had dramatically increased the material standard of living for many in Europe after nearly a millennium of near stagnation for the vast majority of Europeans. The increased generation and distribution of knowledge (i.e., the enlightenment) and the advent of an ever-changing society promised never-ending possibilities following hundreds of years in which "societal change" was viewed by most as impossible and unde-sirable. The new bourgeoisie also advocated for a very limited role for gov-ernment (which had been traditionally associated with aristocratic power) in the economic lives of people. The "invisible hand" of the free market would make life better for everyone (Smith, 1991 [1776]). While elevating the con-cept of individual economic freedom to new heights, the bourgeoisie also pro-moted a rigid set of Christian puritanical moral principles regarding matters such as "proper" gender roles (e.g., patriarchy), interpersonal relations (e.g., honesty, respect), sex (e.g., for the sole purpose of procreation), race, and even manners by which all "true gentlemen" (and ladies) should abide (Elias, 1982). Religion was thus viewed as a form of social control and justification for cap-italism, rather than solely as a means to "find salvation" (Weber, 1998 [1946]).

However, by 1900 it was apparent to nearly everyone that the proposed blessings of liberalism had not fully materialized. Although liberalism and capitalism were presented in universalistic terms, the fruits of this social, eco-nomic, and political ideology, for the most part, went only to the rapidly grow-ing bourgeoisie and those intellectuals and intelligentsia who provided the knowledge necessary for market distribution, research, and development. It was argued that the majority of people (e.g., craftspeople, clergy, serfs) were, in fact, worse off than they had been under feudalism. For example, through-out the middle ages peasants lived at a subsistence level (e.g., hunger and death by disease or starvation was common), had no legal or political rights, and many (particularly women who were accused of witchcraft, and the Jews) suffered from superstition and socio-religious persecution (e.g., Duby, 1968; Holton, 1985; Mollat, 1986). However, as the peasants moved off the land to work in cities, their lot in life did not improve. To the contrary, as Engles (1958 [1845]) recorded, these peasants turned industrial workers (especially women and children who could be hired for less money than adult males) lived in abject poverty, with little or no food, clothing, sanitation, health care, formal education, or housing. These former peasants no longer "belonged" to an estate and were now "free"; however, this freedom resulted in their work-ing extremely long hours in dark, highly polluted and crowded factories for meager wages. In addition, unlike work in the countryside that changed from season to season, these "free" workers found themselves doing mind-numbing, repetitive tasks day in and day out. Disease, crime, exploitation, alienation, and cruelty were rampant under these conditions.

By the twentieth century, it was also clear that the vision of a meritocracy was a myth. Although there was far more social and economic mobility under capitalism than feudalism, those who had managed to create wealth were able to give tremendous advantages to their heirs. Children born into urban poverty had few, if any, opportunities for authentic social and economic mobility, despite their talents or desires. Children born into wealth often would remain affluent whether or not they possessed noteworthy talents or ambition. Due to advantages that the children of the bourgeois and aristocracy had in obtaining education, health care, as well as business and political contacts, the dream of a meritocracy in which everyone had an equal opportunity to live "the good life" turned out to be an illusion.

The reform left represents a split that took place within the bourgeoisie, intellectual, and intelligentsia classes. This split was sparked in response to the gross inequalities of income and rights that was a consequence of what today in the United States would be called laissez-faire capitalism and libertarian politics. In particular, the reformist orientation argued for a more democratically controlled state that would have power to regulate the economy (for purposes of fair competition, employment opportunities, political participation, and broader prosperity) and provide services to promote social justice. Unlike classical liberals and aristocrats who felt poverty should be addressed solely through private charity and "expanding the market," reformists, such as John Hobson (1900, 1920, 1949 [1894], 1971 [1902]), proposed that the state should become a more powerful force for redistributing wealth via a progressive tax structure and use of these taxes for programs to assist workers and their families (e.g., public health, safety, education, unemployment compensation, job training, pensions, sanitation).

Unlike Marx, these reformists, such as John Stuart Mill (1999 [1848]), wanted to keep capitalism for its ability to generate wealth, but similar to Marx, they wanted to ameliorate the problems of poverty and social injustice. Unlike classical liberals and aristocrats, reform leftists wanted to expand democratic control over the state (e.g., universal male suffrage) and increase the power of the state for the promotion of the common welfare of its citizens; however, similar to them, these reformers believed the market and expansion of trade were fundamental requirements of a good society. Contrary to Marxists, they argued that capitalism was needed for the creation of prosperity, but that it must be regulated by the state for the common good.

At the same time, these reformist factions of the bourgeoisie, intellectual, and intelligentsia classes formed an alliance with the rapidly expanding, industrial working class in England. This was a natural collaboration since the workers' movement in England (unlike in Germany) was not dominated by Marxists. These workers did not particularly want to replace capitalism with communism. They did not want to own industries, but rather sought to reform the material (e.g., wages, hours), safety (e.g., lighting, ventilation, hours), and due process (e.g., collective bargaining, arbitration) aspects of industrial labor through participation in democratic politics, collective bargaining, and if necessary, civil disobedience (e.g., public protests, strikes).

Reformers argued that it was in the bourgeoisie's enlightened self-interest to raise workers' standard of living since their increased wealth would prevent revolution and serve as a catalyst for continued economic growth by increasing the number of consumers. Known as the "lib-lab" coalition, these workers, members of the intellectual and intelligentsia classes such as the Fabian Society (Webb, 1901), and their bourgeois allies shared Marx's basic critique of capitalism. That is, if left unregulated, capitalism would create gross inequities and exploitation (at home and abroad) that would eventually lead to violent revolution and the destruction of society. However, this reformist coalition differed significantly from the Marxist response to the crisis of capitalism. Rather than trying to foster a socialist revolution and establish a "dictatorship of the proletariat," the reformist coalition advocated for the creation of a self-critical society in which social problems could be openly identified, and a democratically elected state would be empowered to directly address these problems as they emerged. In this sense, this reformist coalition brought together two powerful ideas. From classical liberalism, it championed the value of individual liberty, private enterprise, and equal justice under written law. From socialism, reformists endorsed the notion that society, as a whole, should assume responsibility for the "common good." Finally, these reformists rejected the religious dogmatism of their liberal predecessors, and advocated for a culture of tolerance regarding the private lives of citizens about such issues as sex, religion, and aesthetics.

While this form of leftist liberalism gained legitimacy in Europe with the social and labor reform policies of Bismark in Germany and Desraeli in England (e.g., Merriman, 1996, Palmer, 1965), its history in the United States was slightly different. One might place the advent of the reformist orientation to the abolition movement in which progressive thinking, male and female members of the African/American, intellectual, intelligentsia, and bourgeoisie classes generated a campaign to end slavery (Buckmaster, 1992). Perhaps the most notable individuals of this coalition included Fredrick Douglas, William Lloyd Garrison, Ralph Waldo Emerson, and Henry David Thoreau (whose essay against U.S. expansionism, "Civil Disobedience," also created a moral foundation for public critique of international policy). After the Civil War, this coalition expanded to include members of the emerging, industrial working class and generated campaigns in support of public education (e.g., Katz, 1968), women's suffrage (Banaszak, 1996), abolishment of child labor and creation of unions (Gourley, 1999; Le Blanc, 1999), ecological conservation (Fox, 1986), and antimonopoly laws (Himmelberg, 1994). Beginning around the turn of the last century and particularly during the 1930s, this coalition generated the labor movement in the United States and reformists achieved power in several spheres of society within the United States (Lichtenstein, 2002). After World War II, many African Americans and women joined this coalition and launched the civil rights and women's liberation campaigns (Storrs, 2000).

This coalition has not always maintained its unity. For example, as previously mentioned, it became badly splintered (i.e., largely due to the defection

of male industrial workers) over the war in Vietnam, the civil rights movement, the ecology campaign, and the women's liberation movement (e.g.,
Rorty, 1998; Isserman and Kazin, 2000). Nevertheless, contemporary
reformists have been associated, for the most part, with attempts to increase
and utilize state power (e.g., Blau, 1999; Gilbert and Gilbert, 1989) through
electoral politics, sociological litigation (Black, 1989), and civil protest
(Buechler, 2000) to regulate the economy (for the purposes of preventing
monopolies, providing near full employment, supporting unions, and fostering small businesses), and redistribute wealth for the purposes of social justice
(e.g., Cumming, 1969; DeLue, 1989; Galbraith, 1958; Hawken et al., 1999;
Keynes, 1926; Rawls, 2001; Sunstein, 1997). This coalition has also been associated with attempts to make our democracy more inclusive, foster greater
awareness and legitimacy of our citizen's diverse ancestral heritages, promote
policies of equitable access into traditionally powerful realms of our society
(e.g., government, business, media services, education), advocate for the secularization of our politics, support the development of an ecologically sustainable economy, defend individual rights and privacy, and resist colonialism and
imperialism. Although the work of the Harmony Education Center is manifested almost exclusively within the educational realm of society, it is best
understood in light of this broader effort to make society as a whole more
democratic and humane.

CONCLUSION: REFLECTIONS ON CHAPTER 2

As previously mentioned, the primary focus of this book concerns the activities of the Harmony Education Center's Office for Outreach Services. Since
its creation, the OOS has worked in hundreds of schools in all parts of the
United States. Their involvement ranges from one-day faculty development
sessions to intensive, multi-year partnerships in which the entire center is
involved (see chapters 3–5). Shortly after the creation of HEC, the Office for
Outreach Services came to the conclusion that these intensive partnerships
offered great potential for fostering substantive school reform, and as a result
we prioritized this type of work between 1990 and 2000. As previously mentioned, during this time, HEC focused many of its efforts in assisting several
"high-poverty" schools.

As previously mentioned, this work is not intended to serve as a "model"
for others to follow. We do not try to illuminate HEC's work for the purpose
of suggesting that therein lies "the answer" to the problems of reforming
schools during this particularly conservative era. In addition, many progressive
organizations are currently operating within the educational realm of our society, and the Harmony Education Center regards itself as merely one of many
participants in this larger tapestry of leftist activity. We now turn our atten-

tion in the next chapter to issues of school autonomy. As will be discussed, the autonomy that individual schools are able to create for themselves is crucial if substantive reforms are to take place in a given building. This is especially true in light of the efforts of people who work primarily in other realms of society, such as the government and economy, to control what happens in our public schools.

Finally, as previously mentioned, the purpose of this book is not to prove some rigid thesis, but rather to state "something clearly enough, intelligibly enough, so that it can be understood and thought about" (Frye, 1983, p. 173). This, of course, stands in sharp contrast to more traditional, quantitative analyses that have been all-too-common in reporting the results of various efforts by school reformers (e.g., Fashola and Slavin, 1998). As many scholars in the field have recently suggested (e.g., Pinar et al., 1995), this type of "autobiographical" scholarship holds great promise for gaining significant understanding into one's work. However, these authors also note that the exploration into one's own life situation can also be extremely fruitful for others engaged in similar activity. Through vicarious experience, one can apply insights drawn from one setting and apply them to another. For example, we have learned much from the work of school reformers and scholars such as Fullan (1993), Glickman (1998), Bullough and Gitlin (1985, 1995), and Talbot and Crow (1998) as well as many others (Hollingsworth, 1997). This book represents a contribution to this relatively small but increasingly significant discourse on school reform based upon the work of those who actually experience it. At the risk of appearing self-serving, it is a discourse we hope will grow larger with time.

The next chapter explores an issue vital to substantive school reform, but that is unfortunately often overlooked by those who are interested in progressive education. As previously mentioned, let us turn our attention to the importance of establishing greater autonomy for schools to make substantive decisions regarding the school environment, personnel, curriculum, and instruction—among other things.

CHAPTER 3

The Local Politics of Educational Reform: Issues of School Autonomy

This chapter represents one area of concern linked to the politics that emerged when, acting as external change agents, HEC became involved in several comprehensive, school-based educational change efforts. While many think of school reform solely in terms of curriculum content, techniques of teaching, and/or classroom management, it is important to remember that much of what goes on during these reform efforts is also political (e.g., Dow, 1991; Mirel, 1994; Muncey and McQuillan, 1992). Local politics refers to the use of formal and informal power by individuals or groups to achieve their goals within a given school (Blase, 1998). As Sarason (1990, p. 7) stated,

> Schools and school systems are political organizations in which power is an organizing feature. Ignore [power] relationships, leave unexamined their rationale, and the existing system will defeat efforts at reform. This will happen . . . because recognizing and trying to change power relationships, especially in complicated, traditional institutions, is among the most complex tasks human beings can undertake.

From this perspective, one of the primary aspects of school reform concerns altering the political relationships and dynamics of power within a given school or district.

Although the school community controls the process, content, and nature of school-based reform, it is not uncommon for external change agents, such as the HEC, to provide guidance and assistance. Fortunately, there is a plethora of scholarship that addresses the processes of this work (e.g., Comer et al., 1996; Elmore, 1990; Fullan, 1993; Glickman, 1993; Hamann, 1992; Murphy, 1991; Sulla, 1998), and more importantly, a small but significant body of knowledge concerning the nature and struggles embedded in these efforts has been recently generated (e.g., Gitlin, 1997; Hatch, 1998; Korostoff, Beck and Gibb, 1998). In an effort to contribute to this latter body of scholarship, this chapter explores the way we, acting as external change agents, and several schools worked through the local

---

*Thanks to Daniel Baron and Carol Myers for their assistance with this chapter.

politics that emerged during school-based reform projects. As its title suggests, the focus of this particular chapter is on issues related to school autonomy. White (1992, p. 69) made an excellent point in stating, "While nearly everyone concerned about education is talking about school restructuring and the need for school-based management, little is known about how school decentralization actually works, how authority is relocated, and how school decentralization affects teachers." Who do schools negotiate with to obtain more autonomy and what issues are the focus of these negotiations? In response to this question, this chapter explores the way in which the dynamics of school autonomy are embedded in several school-based reform projects (see chapter 2), and it will raise a number of issues in light of this reflection.

THE POLITICS OF SCHOOL AUTONOMY

As its name implies, the key principle of school-based reform projects is that the faculty in a given school will have the power to identify, conceptualize, and implement the curricular, instructional, and structural alterations that are deemed necessary to significantly improve students' education. As Bullough and Gitlin (1985, p. 219) stated, educational change has been generally initiated and directed by policymakers and/or district administrators: "Following a model common to many businesses and institutional bureaucracies, school reform efforts have been directed from the top down. That teachers need to be told what to do and how to do it has come almost to be taken for granted." Perhaps in reaction to the failure of such efforts, the notion that significant decisions about educational reform should be made by the people who work on a day-to-day basis with children gained a fair degree of acceptance among educators as well as politicians during the 1990s. In this work, many individuals quickly came to the conclusion that school autonomy was a necessary prerequisite for meaningful school improvement (e.g., Barth, 1990; Darling-Hammond, 1997; Fullan, 1993; Glickman, 1993; Sarason, 1990), and that this shift in power was a central stipulation to the previously mentioned Clinton government's Title I, School-Wide Initiative.

Advocating for and developing a building's autonomy was essential to HEC's work with schools. If schools were not allowed to make substantive decisions regarding the education of the children in their own building, then HEC's involvement wouldn't have been appropriate. However, knowing that school autonomy was a crucial aspect of substantive educational reform, did not mean that it was easy to establish. To the contrary, our work at HEC suggests that there were numerous sources of power and various issues that needed to be resolved if a school was to move towards a more autonomous status.

NEGOTIATING WITH EXTERNAL SOURCES OF POWER

Shank (1994, p. 286) made an excellent point where she stated,

> Autonomy is a concept that institutions define in a variety of ways. Essentially it is a measure of an institution's independence and self-directedness, and the degree to which it is free of interference by outside authority. . . . The greater the school's autonomy, the more it is free from institutional regulation and supervision.

However, it is important to remember that autonomy does not mean that a school can do whatever it wants. A school's autonomy is always a matter of degree, since an individual school must operate within the context of other external powers. Central to negotiating greater school autonomy within a well-established external power structure is the issue of control. That is, who has the power to make what types of decisions that effect the education of children in a particular school? As discussed below, HEC focused much of their work with faculty in helping them understand and negotiate the distribution of power within their districts, and how to increase their realms of control and influence. In this work, schools typically had to negotiate with four external sources of power: district administration, unions, governmental departments of education, and external change agents.

District Administration

One of the most obvious sources of external power were the district administrations in which these various schools existed. As Chubb and Moe (1990) point out, most public schools are legally controlled by locally elected boards that hire professional administrators to manage the operations of their schools. Ultimately, these individuals are responsible for the education in a specific district, and as a result, have a vested interest in what happens in each of their schools. It would have been naïve to think that central administrators would completely abandon their control over what occurred in individual buildings as a result of these school-based reform projects. At the same time, establishing a building's autonomy was so important, it was often the first topic of discussion as HEC began their work:

> Since this district has a reputation of micro-managing their schools, we wanted to clarify the need for building autonomy in today's meeting with the district's Title I coordinator and the assistant superintendent for elementary education. Similar to the other districts in which we work, these individuals believe that school-based reform provides an opportunity to improve the education of their students. They both recognized that over the years there has been a lot of mistrust generated between the "central office" and individual schools. Their main concern was that the education of the children *really* improve. They expected higher scores on the state standardized tests within a few years; however, they

also wanted to see significant "improvement" in the quality of curriculum and instruction, and "more positive" attitudes of both teachers and students towards schooling. They agreed that the schools, themselves, needed to have control over all reforms related to curriculum (content and resources), instructional strategies, internal school governance, building atmosphere, and parent/community relations. This district's administration was so supportive of school-based reform that they mandated (over the next 5 years) that all their high-poverty elementary schools participate in it. The irony of this mandate didn't escape our attention, and it has been subsequently a topic of discussion in our meetings with building faculty. (summary of field notes)

At a minimum, several of the schools with which HEC worked negotiated considerable autonomy over the types and substance of internal reforms that emerged from their deliberations related to curriculum and instruction (e.g., purchasing their own curriculum materials rather than having to use district-wide textbooks; determining topics of study, instructional strategies, and student assessments), internal decision making and structure (e.g., realigning and building a more level hierarchy, creating multiaged versus graded classes, eliminating tracking), use of the building and grounds (e.g., eliminating of classroom desks, creating of gardens), and staff development funds and activities.

In addition, a few schools managed to negotiate power over matters such as hiring new faculty, teacher evaluation, and establishing relationships with district-wide programs (e.g., special education). At times, we were surprised by our success to increase a given school's autonomy in these areas.

This is the third year we've worked with this school. During our meeting today, we discussed the faculty's professional development needs and desire to initiate a "peer evaluation project" of their teaching this year. Towards the end of the discussion, one of the teachers asked, "Wouldn't it be nice to have this [peer evaluation] instead of the usual process [i.e., district supervisor observations and checklist]. After several people affirmed this desire, a decision was made to write a memo to the superintendent asking if this "peer evaluation project" could substitute for the traditional teacher evaluations. Some time was spent discussing the rationale and description of the peer evaluation process to the school's Title I coordinator who volunteered to write the memo. At the end of the meeting, one of the teachers said, "They'll [central administration] never go for it." A week later, the faculty was informed that they would be allowed this substitution, and the only request was that records of its usefulness be kept and thus be treated as a potential "pilot" for the entire district. (summary of field notes)

Another school in a different district proposed the establishment of a "year-round" calendar for their school; but difficulties of student mobility and busing for a single school that was on a different calendar prevented this proposal from becoming realized. Several schools tried to negotiate faculty control over the hiring of building administrators. HEC encouraged these proposals due to the important role principals play in reform efforts.

It's been two months into the second year of reform in this school. Last August we were told that Betty [all proper names are fictitious], the principal, was being transferred to another school in the district. It seems as if this other school needs a really "strong leader" and so the decision was made to transfer Betty there. Whatever the reason, her absence has slowed the pace of reform in this school dramatically. As might have been predicted, the new principal feels unsure of her role and perhaps threatened by the power of the school's leadership team that was created last year. Several teachers told us how the decision to transfer principals confirms their view that central administration doesn't really care about their school, and they resent it. When we discussed this transfer with the district's Title I coordinator, she shrugged her shoulders, rolled her eyes, and mentioned the long history of autocratic control by the central administrators in this district. (summary of field notes)

In spite of advocating for school communities to have an authentic voice in hiring building administrators, only one school, in our many years of work, has been successful. A comment by one administrator helped us understand the difficulty of this goal:

You need to understand. Up until recently, this district had an unwritten policy that principals had to be transferred every three years to keep them from building a strong base of support in the local community and thus be in a position to challenge decisions made by central administrators. Superintendents and their assistants are in a very vulnerable position. If somebody, and it doesn't take a lot of somebodies, doesn't like what's going on in schools, central administrators get the heat. Their only real connection to the schools in their districts is through the principal. They see the principal as *their* representative in the building. It's hard for them to let go of controlling who this representative will be, even if it's ultimately good for the school to have this power for itself.

Given this orientation, it was easy to see the difficulties of expanding a school's autonomy to include the hiring of building administrators.

Negotiating with central administrators over the degree of a school's autonomy is central to the work of substantive school reform. Schools need to know "where they stand" vis-à-vis their district administration. Without overtly addressing these questions of control, educational reformers set themselves up for possible misunderstandings and subsequent frustrations and potential resentments that inevitably arise from these misunderstandings.

Unions

Although most individuals think of central administration juxtaposed against a school's independence, HEC's work found teacher unions to be even more concerned about the implications of school autonomy. This perception is not unique. Unions have, at times, been portrayed as the primary obstacle to improving the education of young people. Some school reformers have called for a complete reassessment of union representation, even going so far as to call for an end to collective bargaining, under the auspices of "school restructuring" (e.g., Brimelow, 2003; Casner-Lotto, 1988; Chubb and Moe, 1990; Finn and Clements, 1989; Lieberman, 2000). Our experience, however, suggests that these proposals have been unwarranted.

In the school districts in which we worked, the unions were not a bulwark against school autonomy, but union resistance might have occurred if we failed to negotiate our school reform plans with their representatives. Unlike central administrators who were chiefly interested in controlling certain decisions such as the hiring and removal of building principals, unions in these districts focused their concerns primarily on protecting teachers' work loads:

> Today we met with union representatives from both the school building and district. Unlike in Merryville where the union and district administration have developed a collaborative relationship, the union and management in Sharptown have had a long history of distrust and conflict. Four years ago, this community had a bitter and protracted teachers' strike that damaged both the union and school board/administration, and there continues to be significant mistrust between these groups. As the meeting began, we soon learned that the union was particularly concerned about reform efforts that would require teachers to work extra hours without compensation. From their perspective, schools that had "gone school-based" in the previous two years seemed to expect their teachers to volunteer hours during the process of reform. We did not deny that some teachers had volunteered their time. After all, authentic change requires that teachers study and communicate with their colleagues on a regular basis, and we understood the difficulty of finding time to do this during the academic year. As we further explored each other's concerns and desires for improving the education of the children, we reached an understanding. The contract stipulates that teachers must be available for an hour every day after school, but each school could (with faculty approval) alter the scheduling of these hours so that a block of time could be set aside for reform work. Another concern of the union was that teachers might be expected to assume administrative responsibilities (such as a newly created position of "team leader") without recognition or compensation for these new responsibilities. We responded by saying that no structural changes would occur in any building unless the faculty reached consensus on it. Given this understanding, the representatives agreed that any specific aspect of the current contract could be waived if 90 percent of the teachers in a given building agreed to the change. As we talked more, the union representatives' concern that these efforts would weaken their members dissipated. (summary of field notes)

This concern for protecting teachers' work loads was a potential, but not a necessary obstacle for reform. However, it required schools to develop creative schedules. For example, the teachers in one school decided to start work 30 minutes early each day of the week, provide extra curricular activities for the students who could not leave early, and thus freed Wednesday afternoons for the faculty to engage in school reform work. In another school, the faculty decided to leave school immediately after class on Fridays, but stayed for two hours on Thursday for reform discussions. A third school met once each week after school for two hours, but gave each faculty member the option of leaving after the first hour.

Another major concern of unions was seniority. In particular, questions of hiring and transferring faculty between schools became potentially problematic:

> In our discussion with the principal today, we emphasized the importance of hiring future teachers that will agree with the new values and vision of the school. If newly hired teachers do not agree with these values and vision, then it would be difficult to fully implement the school's plans for change. We also encouraged him to give his faculty a voice in hiring any new teachers. He responded that he had little or no choice in selecting new faculty. The contract between the union and the school board stipulated that he could only hire a new faculty member if no teachers already employed by the district wanted to transfer to his school. He only had a choice if more than one teacher requested a transfer to fill a position. Only if no one requested a transfer could he hire a new teacher from outside the district, and in those situations, all the principals who needed faculty met to decide (or as this principal told us "compete") over which candidates were offered a job in which buildings. (summary of field notes)

Protecting the jobs of union members was central to its mission, and one cannot criticize the union for negotiating these types of policies into their contract. However, under certain circumstances, it was very possible for a school to be prevented from selecting their own colleagues which we viewed as a highly desirable goal. These schools spent considerable time and effort generating the ideas and values upon which their alterations were based. If schools could not select future teachers who shared these ideas and values, then it placed the long-term possibilities for substantive reform in jeopardy. However, no school with which we have worked during the 1990s was successful in negotiating a hiring process that replaced seniority with educational ideology or talent as a basis for hiring or transferring teachers.

Although contract policies can limit a school's autonomy, it is important to remember that unions have played a meaningful role in the development of our nation's education (Murphy, 1990; Urban, 1982). In many situations they have advocated for progressive policies such as collective bargaining, the equalization of pay between male and female teachers, limits on class size (a major issue of negotiation in one of the districts in which we worked), health and pension benefits, safety regulations, tenure, and grievance procedures. On the other hand, teacher unions have also succumbed to conservative and at times even reactionary stances such as the expulsion of "communist" members during the red scare of the late 1940s and early 1950s, and its resistance to "community control of schools" as in the Ocean Hill-Brownsville conflict in 1968. These latter tensions still exist in many urban areas, and as illustrated above, emerged in our work with schools.

The issue of teacher unions and school autonomy is complex. Teacher unions historically have followed the structure and interests of the industrial trade union movement. That is, the welfare of their members supersedes the production of a company's product. Although it is not difficult to value the lives of workers over the production of an object, teacher unions occasionally seem to pit the welfare of their members over the welfare of a community's children. These conflicting interests often emerged as altercations among the faculty in several of the schools in which we worked (see chapter 4).

Government

Another external power which placed limits on these schools' autonomy was the federal and state departments of education. For instance, each school was required by law to follow curricular, safety, equal access, and other regulations established by the state legislature. Several years prior to our involvement with these schools, these regulations clearly served as a fetter against a school establishing more building autonomy. In response to the 1980's calls for reform, many state departments of education published lists of essential reading, writing, and math skills for each grade level and required students to take a competency test for these skills. Unlike standardized competency exams in the past that were used for individual assessment by the teacher and student, these reforms initiated what several scholars called "high-stakes" tests, in that a school's scores are made public, and state funding was partially determined by the scores children received on them (e.g., Herman and Golan, 1993; Madaus, 1990; Shepard and Doughty, 1991; Vinson, Gibson and Ross, 2001).

As these scholars noted, high-stakes competency tests have significantly narrowed the range of potential curriculum and instructional strategies that might be explored by a school or teacher. Specifically, these exams focused the content of schools on discreet minimum skills through drill work and practice testing. In districts where HEC has worked, these regulations were interpreted in ways that left little room for meaningful classroom and/or school-based curricular development. In response to the state's regulations, district administrators bought comprehensive instructional programs specifically designed to raise children's scores on these standardized tests. These programs came complete with all materials needed for instruction (often including written dialogue of what teachers should say to students), step-by-step lessons for each day and each "subject" (i.e., skill area), individualized worksheets for remediation of particular skills, review lessons and quizzes, and tests (that could often be graded by computers).

Given this orientation, several observers noted that during the 1980s elementary teachers became increasingly "deskilled" (e.g., Apple and Teitelbaum, 1986; Frymier, 1987; Goodman, 1988; Myers, 1986; Shannon, 1987; Woodward, 1986). Instead of viewing teachers as reflective practitioners who are capable of establishing a relevant and meaningful education for their students, these instructional programs transformed educators into little more than instructional technicians who merely coordinated the day's work to ensure that students "get through the material" on time. During the last two decades, most staff development in schools has focused on helping teachers become more efficient at managing these programs.

Perhaps due to the limited success of these instructional programs, the districts in which we worked (especially those located in high poverty areas) were open to other options including classroom and/or school-based curriculum development as a way to improve their students' education. As a result, these schools were no longer required to use these instructional programs if they found or developed more promising curricula for their students. However, teaching the "essential skills" and scoring well on the state standardized test was still extremely important in the minds of district and building administrators, the school boards, and teachers:

> We were discussing the rationale for this school's reform and Betty mentioned improving the children's scores on the state's test. "I know there are more important things about education than this test. I know it doesn't measure everything or even the most important things children need to know in life. I know that the test is biased in many ways and too much emphasis is placed on it. But it's a reality we all have to live with. I hate that they now give the test at the beginning of the year. I know the scores aren't a reflection of what I do with them in class, but it's my name that gets listed when they publish the class scores, and so getting these scores up is damn important to me." (summary of field notes)

Many individuals similarly spoke of "pressure" to improve the children's scores, and expected that any reform efforts would eventually result in higher test scores. Of course, with the passing of No Child Left Behind legislation, this pressure has only increased. The concern of being rated a "failing" school has created an atmosphere of fear and intimidation in some of the schools in which HEC has worked, making our efforts even more challenging.

Several states had other regulations besides the standardized test and the listing of skills to be taught in each grade such as the number of days in each academic year, minimum number of minutes devoted to each subject per week, and minimum teacher–child ratio. While several of the schools where we worked received waivers from many of these regulations (e.g., minutes per subject), none were able to obtain a waiver from taking the state's standardized test.

As might be expected, we engaged the faculty in numerous discussions about testing and skill-focused curriculum in these schools. Ironically, one government regulation that came with Title I school-wide funding during the Clinton administration assisted faculty in reconsidering the value of a skills-based curriculum. Throughout the 1990s, the federal government's Title I school-based reform guidelines primarily addressed issues of the reform process (i.e., conducting a comprehensive needs assessment of the school, developing long-term educational goals, identifying strategies needed to reach these goals, planning staff development activities, and establishing a process for yearly assessment); however, one regulation did address the issue of academic skills. Specifically, this regulation reflected the influence of Dr. Henry Levin's ideas concerning accelerated education and stated that essential skills should be taught in "an enriched and accelerated curriculum." This statement, along with the fact that children's test scores improved in each of the schools after reforms were implemented, provided faculty with a powerful basis for not automatically associating higher scores on standardized tests with a skills-based curriculum.

Although discussions that examined the value of skills-based curriculum and drill-based instruction were significant, the issue of a faculty's perceived power has, in HEC's experience, been even more important in helping faculty reconsider external regulations. In each school, faculty expressed sentiments indicating an extreme lack of efficacy. Faculty often verbalized their skepticism that "they" (e.g., central administrators, the state) will allow them to plan and implement their own reforms, or as one teacher stated, "You're telling us we can chart our own course? I'll believe it when I see it." It is important to remember that these faculty, especially in high-poverty schools, are used to being told what to do. Each year brought with it new "reforms" (e.g., Assertive Discipline, Math Your Way, Reading Recovery, Daily Oral Reading, Success for All), what one principal called the "program de jour," stipulated by the school district or the state Department of Education to implement. Over the years, any sense of efficacy seems to have atrophied among the faculty in most of these schools.

Nevertheless, in most of the schools where HEC worked, the power of the state's "high-stakes" test, list of grade level skills, and the difficulty of knowing who to talk to about these governmental regulations greatly under-mined the autonomy a school might potentially obtain. One might rightfully question if any meaningful school autonomy could take place given the power of tests and skills lists to determine what (and how) content should be taught. However, after much discussion, many of these schools found the civic courage to move substantially away from, as one teacher stated, "the skill, drill, and kill" practices that had prevailed in these schools for well over a decade.

External Change Agents

A final outside power with whom the schools needed to negotiate in develop-ing their autonomy were the external change agents such as those in HEC. As previously mentioned, most of these schools have had a plethora of "staff developers" come into their schools in an effort, as one teacher stated, "to fix us. They come, do their thing, and then leave. They don't really understand us or our kids. All they really care about is whatever they happen to be pushing [instructional program]." Anyon (1997) correctly points out that many faculty, especially in high-poverty schools, are extremely weary and suspicious of these "outsiders."

Several of our inaugural activities helped mitigate these initial attitudes of distrust. In our first meetings with a given school community, we clearly explained the intensive partnership being offered by HEC, and in particular, our roles as facilitators and informed participants in the reform project. Throughout these meetings, we were extremely sensitive to the negative history of staff developers being hired to "change schools" and overtly expressed our desire not to impose a particular "model" of education on the school. The school community was given assurance that they will be the people who will determine the reforms necessary to create the school they wanted. In the high-poverty schools that were told by their central administrators that they must go through this reform project, we spent considerable time with the school community discussing ways to make the process as meaningful as possible given the irony of the mandate.

These initial meetings were helpful in establishing a tentative working relationship between HEC and the school community; however, trust often did not begin to develop until we conducted the previously mentioned ethnographic interviews. Although the interviews were structured around a few "grand tour questions," as stated in chapter 2, what emerged from them were the stories of a school. Each member of a school community had a story to tell, and in telling it to us, often for the very first time, trust slowly developed. At the end of our interviews, several teachers expressed sentiments similar to Martha's: "I never realized how much [frustration] was built up in me. Just talking about it, finally, I feel like a big weight has been lifted from my shoulders." This trust was often deepened when we shared our findings with the school community, which were filled with quotes (anonymous) from the interviews. At the conclusion of these reports, it was not uncommon for someone to say something similar to this teacher's comment: "Well, one thing for sure, you really know who we are and what this school is like." The rapport developed through these interviews helped us overcome much of the historical antipathy faculty feel about external change agents.

However, this early rapport did not completely resolve the issue. At some point in the process, and in nearly every school in which we worked, there came a time when our motives and even our integrity were questioned by at least a few members of the school community. In one school this challenge came from a school administrator, in another from a few teachers, and in another from a parent or concerned community member. Whenever our involvement with a given school was contested, we found it best to deal with it directly:

Dorothy, the school's Title I coordinator, called us last night extremely upset. It seems as if a few of the teachers have been questioning the legitimacy of our partnership with their school. In response, we altered the agenda for tomorrow's meeting with the faculty so we could discuss these teachers' concerns as the first item for discussion. We began the meeting by stating, "Recently we heard through the grapevine that some of the faculty had some questions about our involvement with the school, and before we continue with the work, we felt it important to address any concerns you or someone you know might have about us, our role, or anything else." After a minute or two of silence, finally one of the teachers said, "Several teachers were wondering who is paying you for your time. Is it the school?" We explained that about 50 percent of the funds were coming from the state's Title I School-Wide Initiative and the rest from district and local funding agencies. As we continued explaining the details, one teacher asked how much we were earning as "consultants," and they were surprised that we earned less than many of them. They wanted to know why we would want to work in their school. As one person asked, "What are you getting out of it?" We reiterated what we told them at our first meeting several months ago. Namely, our motives were, for the most part, ideological. "Like you, we want to do what we can to help improve the education of children, especially children who are marginalized in our society." We once again told them the history and the reasons why the Harmony Education Center was established in the first place. After about an hour, the discussion ended with us applauding them for raising these questions. "In lots of schools, teachers wouldn't say anything, but would instead be resentful and angry with us. Discussing these types of issues, no matter how difficult, is better than the alternative [keeping silent and getting angry or frustrated]." We concluded by encouraging them to raise these or any other concerns they might have about our work with them in public or private. (summary of field notes)

After this conversation and others like it, our emotional connection to the school often became deeper. Our willingness to deal with these types of issues increased the level of trust and commitment between HEC and the school communities. As a result, we, ironically, came to value having our motives and integrity questioned by the school community.

At times, the politics associated with our involvement with a given school were more complex and highly charged. As we will see in the next chapter, one of the major, initial problems facing many of these schools was the prevalence of growing antagonism. In all but one or two schools in which we worked, the school community was divided into conflicting factions. As the case below illustrates, it was difficult, at times, to avoid being caught between these competing factions.

Jane, the principal and a strong advocate for children, asked for this meeting with us and the district's Title I coordinator to discuss our role in her school. During our initial interviews at Jane's school, we became aware of the deep hostility between Jane (and her supporters) and a group of teachers in the building who were very active in the union. From the various stories we heard, it seems that when Jane became principal last year she did so with a great deal of fanfare about "improving" or "fixing" Bradley Elementary School. Several teachers believed that Jane implied that the teachers in this school were not working hard or knew how to teach low-income children. During her first year as principal, this group of teachers filed numerous "grievances" against her. In response, Jane eventually filed a law suit against these teachers for harassment. In this meeting Jane accused us of either being allies with this group of teachers or being "used" by them to take control of the school, and thus wanted to end our partnership. She described several situations that she felt illustrated her concerns. Fortunately, we were able to indicate to her how our actions in these circumstances were either a result of simple misunderstandings or poor communication, and agreed to several changes in our work to avoid these problems in the future. More importantly, we were able to help her see the benefits (e.g., higher level of commitment from teachers to reform, sense of ownership and pride in the school, accountability for the education of their children, resolution of conflicts) that comes from distributing power more equally in the school through the establishment of a leadership team and study groups. (summary of field notes)

Although Jane's concerns were resolved in this meeting, in another school in which there was extreme mistrust, disrespect, and animosity between most of the teachers and the principal, we were not able to maintain our neutrality. As we began to establish structures such as a leadership team and rituals (e.g., feedback norms, standards of communication, consensus decision making) to democratize and redistribute power in the building, our involvement was terminated by the principal (see chapter 4).

In summary, we have learned that our position as external change agents cannot be taken for granted. It would be naïve to think that we could request from a given school community a year or more of hard work, the redistribution of power, a serious study and thoughtful reconsideration of their students' education, and the implementation of a comprehensive plan to improve this education and not have our status and function, at some point in the process, questioned and challenged.

CONCLUSION: REFLECTIONS ON CHAPTER 3

As previously mentioned, many educators consider school autonomy to be one of the fundamental components needed to initiate and sustain authentic reform of our children's education. Our experience as external, educational change agents during the 1990s tended to support this contention. Until school communities are given the authority to make significant decisions regarding the education of their children, they will not take the responsibility necessary to improve it. However, recognizing the value of school autonomy does not automatically result in its manifestation. We have learned that issues of autonomy must be addressed whenever they emerge in the process of reforming schools, and our goal in such moments is to help people work through these issues, rather than win or lose battles. If the status of a school's autonomy cannot be resolved in a manner that all parties can honestly accept, then the work of improving the education of children is extremely difficult. Although it was crucial to openly confront these issues whenever they arose, we found it even more important to find "common ground" from which people could work together in good faith and thus minimize any unnecessary conflict. The autonomy of a school needs to be worked through rather than resolved in ways that leave some people as victorious and others vanquished. As we reflect upon our own experiences as portrayed in this chapter, we are left with several matters worthy of continued contemplation.

The first matter concerns the definition of organizational autonomy. Some imply that only individuals can claim to be autonomous, and that institutions by their nature cannot exercise autonomous action (Gaylin and Jennings, 1996). If autonomy is not applicable to organizations then much of our work may be futile. However, as Kant (1959 [1785]) noted, autonomy is a state of potential existence available all "free rational agents," that is, beings or subjects who are capable of rational thought, informed decision making, and moral empathy (i.e., the categorical imperative). He also pointed out that organizations, institutions, and even nations are best viewed as a collective subject or being and thus qualify under his previous definition (Cassirer, 1981). From this perspective, it is useful to view organizational autonomy as a state of mind. Like individuals who wish to be autonomous, we found that schools must struggle to develop a sense of confidence and self-reliance in a political environment (see chapter 1) that distrusts what happens in "schools," particularly those located in high-poverty communities. Given this conception, organizational autonomy is not an object that can be just "given" to a school nor does it appear like magic from the sky. Similarly, autonomy is not an "event" that takes place in a moment of time where one minute an organization lacks autonomy and the next it has it. To the contrary, developing a school's autonomy takes time and effort. School autonomy is, in part, a function of collective cognition and perception. Our experience suggests that until a given school community no longer sees itself as victimized by the numerous constraints and problems it typically must face (see chapter 4), it will not generate the sense of efficacy to effectively confront those in superordinate positions of power.

As Kant (1959 [1785]) notes, and as we have illustrated in this chapter, autonomy is not synonymous with license or the freedom to do whatever one wants or what several social theorists refer to as "negative freedom" (Gaylin and Jennings, 1996). Rather, to be autonomous means to be self-ruled or self-governed. It connotes that one has the aptitude to establish values, rules of conduct based upon those values, and the self-discipline to act accordingly (Cassirer, 1981). An autonomous individual or organization does not have the license to act without regard to the impact that actions might have on other potential free-rational agents. From this perspective, autonomy is a state of power that can only really exist in relation to other subjects (individuals and/or organizations) who operate within the same legal domain. Autonomous schools must learn how to negotiate with others who have power and responsibility for the education of our children. In our work, schools typically negotiated with their district administrators, union representatives, state (and in some schools, federal) government workers, and ourselves, as external change agents. As we've discussed, these negotiations often focused on issues of curricular content and materials, instructional strategies and learning activities, internal governance, work loads, hiring procedures, the role of external change agents, evaluations of children and teachers, and staff development. Although we have begun to explore the nature and substance of these negotiations in our own work, additional scholarship is sorely needed. In particular, because we assumed the power necessary to set up a democratic structure and decision-making process needed to initiate the task of reforming a given school's culture (see chapter 4) and openly shared our views on numerous issues related to the education of children as the work evolved, we would find additional scholarship that explores the negotiations between openly ideological external change agents and school communities especially beneficial (see chapter 6).

Finally, it is extremely important to emphasize that increasing a given school's autonomy will not automatically improve the education of children. It is not hard to imagine a school gaining more power and using this power unwisely. School autonomy is a crucial first step in a very long journey. However, without seriously attending to the issue of school autonomy, reformers may very well undermine the difficult work involved in substantively improving the education of our children. Once a school's autonomy has been more comprehensively established, we can turn our attention to the distribution of power within a particular building. In the next chapter, therefore, an analytical portrayal of the democratic rituals and structures that were generated in these schools is presented. These structures and rituals serve as a foundation upon which substantive educational decisions regarding the schooling of children can be fostered.

CHAPTER 4

Constructing a Democratic Foundation for School-Based Reform Discourse

As stated in the last chapter, increasing a school's organizational autonomy will not automatically improve the education of children or the quality of teachers' work in a given building. Although school autonomy is a crucial first step in a very long journey, it is equally important to help schools create a democratic ethos and "culture" within which to generate pedagogical and curricular reform conversations. As Anderson (1998, p. 572) observed, the notion that decisions about educational reform should be made by the people who work on a day-to-day basis with children has gained some acceptance in the United States:

> Viewed in education as an antidote to entrenched bureaucracy, hierarchy, and excessive specialization, [school-based reform] appears to have strong support among superintendents, principals, teachers, and the general public, regardless of their political ideologies.

However, Anderson (1998) and others point out that school-based reform is extremely challenging (e.g., Anderson and Grinberg, 1998; Barker, 1993; Campbell and Neill, 1994; Campbell and Southworth, 1990; Katz, 1995; Hargraves, 1994; Lipman, 1997).

ESTABLISHING DEMOCRATIC STRUCTURES AND RITUALS

Although creating democratic structures, rituals, and ethos as a foundation upon which school-reform discourse can emerge in a given school is difficult, we were surprised at the positive response we received in nearly every school in which HEC worked. Our portrayal of these efforts might best be presented around three goals that emerged from our work: 1) establishing democratic governance, 2) promoting the voices in a given school community, and 3) providing ways to work through conflict. Following this discussion, we explore several issues that emerged in light of our work as external educational change agents committed to improving the education of children within a democratic ethos.

---

*Thanks to Daniel Baron and Carol Myers for their assistance with this chapter.

Democratic Governance

At the heart of school-based reform is the disruption of conventional ways that power is distributed within a given building. In most of the schools in which we worked, official power flowed from the principal down to teachers and staff, and then to students and their parents. However, like in all complex organizations, the flow of power was more multifaceted than the previous statement would imply. One of the common themes that emerged during our introductory interviews was the fact that all of these schools, to some degree, were "loosely coupled systems" (Weick, 1988). Either by direct opposition with the assistance of their unions or through indirect noncompliance, subordinates in these schools often found ways to ignore or alter many superordinate directives. However, without exception, the vast majority of faculty especially in high-poverty schools initially expressed deep feelings of powerlessness. Several faculty expressed similar sentiments as Beverly, a fourth grade teacher with nineteen years of experience, "I'll believe it [the faculty having an authentic role in reforming her school] when I see it. This school can't change. A year from now you [Harmony Education Center] will be a distant memory" (excerpt from introductory interview).

Given this situation, we found it necessary to set up a structure to maximize participation in all aspects of the reform project. Ironically, the power to establish this structure was given to us initially for being the project "facilitators." The governance restructuring that took place in Elletstown Elementary School was similar to what occurred in each of the schools where we worked:

> Once the introductory interviews were completed and the findings reported to the faculty, the building administrators (e.g., principal, assistant principal, Title I coordinator), teachers, parents, and support staff formed a Leadership Team (LT). We suggested the following criteria to the principal for selecting teachers: 1) willingness to work, 2) grade-level representation, and 3) diverse representation regarding race, gender, age, and seniority in the building/profession. At the first LT meeting, we explained that its primary responsibility was to encourage, articulate, communicate, and coordinate the ideas of the school community, and we then asked if anyone else should be included. A few suggestions were made, and the principal agreed to ask these individuals to join. At our first meeting with the entire faculty, the LT was introduced, and we asked each teacher to internally identify at least one individual on the LT who they trusted to represent their interests. If a given faculty member did not feel represented, s/he was invited to join or recommend someone else who would have his/her trust. One teacher accepted our invitation. (summary of field notes)

The question of who participates in making school-reform decisions, however, cannot be fully satisfied through representative governance.

As many educational change agents have noted, unless faculty are directly involved in making the reforms for their school, the likelihood of noncompliance and/or sabotage is greatly increased (e.g., Anderson, 1998; Barth, 1990;

Fullan, 1993; Glickman, 1993; Sarason, 1990). In addition, given the complexity of school-based reform, ideas from the entire school community are essential. Therefore, in addition to the LT, Study Groups (SG), similar to those at Westview Elementary, were created in each school where we worked.

> Today's LT agenda was to identify topics [based on a collective analysis of the introductory interviews and several structured dialogues with the school community] to be studied in preparation for writing the school's vision and reform plan. After a lengthy conversation, the LT generated three SGs: 1) Curriculum, Instruction, and Assessment, 2) Student/Parent Empowerment, and 3) School Climate. Members of the LT then selected which SG they wanted to join, making sure there was at least two members of the LT team on each SG for the purpose of coordinating ideas and minimizing duplication of work. At the next faculty meeting, each individual joined one of the SGs. The LT explained that the SGs would generate proposals rather than establish regulations to be imposed upon their colleagues. The SGs' primary purpose was to study (e.g., read and discuss relevant literature, make site visits to Harmony and other schools, arrange for discussions with individuals who have special knowledge of their topic). Once their inquiry was completed, each SG would generate one or two goals and several specific strategies for each goal to be included in the school's reform plan. The LT ended by asking the SGs to increase their membership (e.g., parents, community volunteers, students, support staff) who might be interested in the topic. (summary of field notes)

Through the establishment of these SGs, each member of the school community had the opportunity to directly influence the type of school they wanted to see emerge from the project.

Although creating a democratic structure to enhance the potential participation of the school community in reforming the education and culture of their building was essential, it was not viewed as the ultimate goal. Significant reform was best manifested in schools that, along with the above structure or one similar to it, established ways of making decisions through which members of the community were not just physically present, but who felt as if their ideas were heard and valued. As a result, we built upon the previously described structure, and established a ritual of decision making in these schools that maximized the voices of the school community.

Expanding Voices

Being represented or even physically present at meetings does not automatically translate into an experience of being heard. Faculty meetings have a long history of inattention by those present. In addition, individuals rarely speak their minds in these meetings. If they disagree with what is being said, the usual reaction is to remain quiet, and either become apathetic, resentful, and/or ridicule the idea with one's colleagues once the meeting is adjourned.

> The thing that has changed the most is that we really talk to each other now. Before, when we had meetings nobody listened. If something was said you didn't like, you kept quiet and put it down afterwards to your friends. (Follow-up interview, fourth grade teacher)

We heard similar comments from faculty in each of the schools at the end of their planning year. In order to contest this culture of silence, it was necessary to engage in several strategies.

Perhaps the most important response to such a culture of silence is to ensure that everyone has an opportunity to speak and be heard. To meet this challenge, we encouraged schools to have those individuals who were directly affected by a particular decision to have an unmediated voice in making that decision. To facilitate this goal, we encouraged school communities to make decisions by a consensus defined in similar ways as at Yellowspring Elementary:

> Before a decision becomes policy, a call for consensus will be made. You can consent to a decision if you can say "yes" to the following questions: 1) I can "live" with the decision, that is, the implementation of this recommendation does not make working in this school impossible for me, 2) I will enthusiastically support those colleagues who want to act on this recommendation even if I am not excited about it myself, 3) I will do nothing to subvert this decision once it has been agreed upon. Before calling for consensus, we will ask for questions, comments, or concerns. This call provides one last opportunity to voice your opinions. If subsequently you have misgivings about a decision, you can always bring it up in future meetings. In fact, all decisions will be regularly reviewed, so there will always be opportunities to raise concerns. Before a recommendation that impacts everyone can become school policy it must obtain consensus from the appropriate SG, then it goes to the LT, and if the LT reaches consensus, it finally goes to the whole faculty. If the LT cannot reach consensus, then the recommendation goes back to the SG with suggested alterations from the LT. This continues until both groups reach consensus. [At this point someone asked why not just vote and let the majority rule.] From our experience, the problem with voting is that someone always ends up losing, and potentially this feeling of loss can too easily lead to subversion of the decision through noncompliance or worse. (summary of field notes)

As a school community became familiar with consensus decision making, it learned to treat disagreements and problems as concerns to work through, rather than dividing lines around which cliques fight.

> The purpose of today's retreat is to review and approve all of the proposed goals and strategies that have emerged from the SGs and the LT. The final approval of the reform plan went smoothly with one exception. One goal was to engage students in more intellectually challenging activities, and the proposed strategy was to teach at least one lesson each day that calls upon students to use their powers of observation, speculation, analysis, synthesis,

and/or imagination. At this point, the three first grade teachers did not consent to the proposal. When asked why, they pointed out their responsibilities to "teach the basics," which left no time to teach these lessons, and that young children could not easily engage in these types of intellectual activities. Several teachers questioned such assertions. One teacher stated, "We're not talking about a complete revamping of your curriculum. Certainly, you could find time to do a science experiment, something as simple as having students observe what happens to an ice cube when placed on a plate in the room. The kids could keep notes of what happens, speculate on why it happens, and discuss their speculations, couldn't they?" After several exchanges, the first grade teachers were still not convinced. As a result, the plan was altered to exclude the first grade teachers from agreeing to participate in this particular strategy. After the plan was changed, consensus was reached. (summary of field notes)

Making decisions by consensus minimized the likelihood of teachers' noncompliance to or subversion of agreed-upon actions. Commitments made under this process generally seemed to be taken seriously by each school community. Most importantly, consensus decision making avoided feelings of exclusion and of being silenced, which occurs to those who are on the losing side of a given vote. Once a school begins making decisions by consensus, it often provides skeptical faculty with new hope.

I think the turning point came with the resolution of the paper crisis. [He was asked to explain]. After about a month of school, the principal unilaterally told us we could no longer take any paper from the storage room. Some teachers, she claimed, had used too much causing this "crisis." Several teachers were so upset that they wanted to file a grievance against her. It seemed like the principal was hoarding paper and only giving it to those teachers she felt were "worthy." At Carol's request, the teachers held off on filing the grievance and turned the matter over to the LT. The LT created a committee composed of teachers who were perceived as the principal's "friends and foes" to study the problem and recommend a solution to the LT with the stipulation that any solution had to be reached by consensus. About a month later, the LT met with this committee to discuss their recommendations, and after several minor modifications reached consensus on this proposal. The following week, the full faculty met to discuss the recommendations, and they, too, reached consensus. I've been working at this school for 15 years, and this was the first time we ever collectively made a decision about anything. When I first heard about this [school reform], I was doubtful, but maybe something good will come of it after all. (summary of informal conversation)

It took time to teach a school community how to operate by consensus; however, as one teacher stated in a follow-up interview, "Making decisions this way, makes working here much better. This is the first job I've had where I felt that what I say really counts" (follow-up interview).

In addition to making decisions by consensus, we discovered that the individual voices of a school community need to be actively sought out. Overtly seeking ideas from individuals is rarely found in schools or discussed in reform literature. Faculty with whom we have worked were unaccustomed to seeking out the ideas of their colleagues, or having requests made for their input into discussions. In virtually every school, we incorporated this type of activity into our work. Our efforts to elicit ideas took place in several different contexts.

First, our introductory interviews (see chapter 2) provided an opportunity for each school community member to articulate his or her ideas and concerns. As previously stated, these half-hour interviews established a precedent for school community members to "speak their minds." In reporting the findings from these interviews, we read numerous quotes. (Each interviewee was told that their comments will remain anonymous, but not confidential.) As a result, faculty, often for the very first time in their careers, actually heard their voices and the voices of their colleagues. "The first thing that impressed me [about the school's reform project] was hearing everyone's comments when Carol reported the results of the interviews. Just hearing what people really thought about the school, the kids, and what we are doing here got to me" (follow-up interview with a third grade teacher). Emphasizing the right to be heard was central to our work in these schools.

> Ms. Randolf, a black third grade teacher, was speaking. After a couple of minutes, we noticed that a small group of Euro-American teachers were whispering, rather than listening. After she finished talking, Daniel said, "Something that just happened reminded me of a conference session I attended on African American issues in education. I was the only white person, and before the session started, someone asked if I should stay. This person explained that often when Whites and Blacks are in a discussion, whites tend to dominate the conversation. When Blacks do speak, their comments are ignored, and if a white person later makes the same point, people then respond. I was allowed to stay, but was reminded that this particular session was to give Blacks an opportunity to speak. I told you this story because I noticed that a group of teachers weren't paying attention to Ms. Randolf while she was speaking, and it reminded me of that session. One of the things we need to work on is creating an atmosphere in which everyone's voice is heard." After the meeting was over, Daniel spoke to the white teachers who had been whispering, and asked them if they were offended by what he had said. Ms. Arnold replied, "God, no. As a special education teacher, I often feel the regular education teachers don't pay attention when I speak. It [listening to each other] is something we really do need to establish as a norm." (summary of field notes)

A second context occurred in meetings. Specifically, we often asked individuals who were silent for their comments, and when concerns come to our attention, we encouraged public disclosure.

The Parent Coordinator (PC) asked us to help her with a parent who was convinced that her child's teacher was racist. She accused the teacher of denigrating him and other black children in the class. The teacher was White and the only children who received her verbal belittlement were Black. When the parent confronted the teacher, she denied the accusation. The parent felt as if the teacher was completely unresponsive to her concerns. PC was not sure how to proceed. We suggested she invite the parent to speak with (and perhaps even join) the Parent Involvement Study Group [of which the PC was a member]. We suggested that at this time, not to single the teacher out, but to work with the SG and to develop some goals that would help minimize the likelihood that teachers would continue to respond to parents in this fashion and to plan some strategies to explore the dynamics of racial differences between teachers, students, and parents. We also suggested that she begin to keep records of parents' concerns regarding the way this teacher interacts with her black students, in case a direct confrontation would be necessary at a later date. We also suggested that she try to establish a working relationship with this teacher to develop trust as the basis for giving her more direct feedback about this or other situations that might emerge in the future. (summary of field notes)

In most public schools, when individuals become aware of situations that need alteration, they often do not have a structure through which their voice can be heard. After many years of working in these types of schools, people forget that they have a voice.

A final context for seeking out voices occurred during brief and unplanned occasions. Whenever possible, we consciously reached out to those community members who rarely spoke. During breaks or after a given meeting, we asked individuals who had been silent for feedback regarding what had been said by various colleagues. If the feedback seemed significant, we encouraged them to articulate their ideas at the next opportunity. In those cases in which one had reason to remain silent, we offered to share their ideas anonymously. In addition, we visited each classroom and established student leadership teams as a way to facilitate children's voices in reforming their schools.[1] Helping people "find their voice" was central to our work. If and when we noticed members of a given school community seeking out each other's ideas, we knew that this school was well on its way to establishing a foundation for substantive reform discourse.

Confronting Conflict

Our final goal towards establishing a school culture in which substantive educational reform can be fostered was to make it possible for a given school to work through its differences in public and in ways that minimize the potential for subsequent feelings of marginalization and the sabotage that often accompanies conflicts. One of the central problems facing many of these schools was the existence of building antagonisms. For example, in one school the faculty was divided between the upstairs (grades 4–6) and the downstairs (grades K–3).

> Before we began working on this [reform project], the upstairs and downstairs [teachers] wouldn't speak to each other. The upstairs thought the downstairs did nothing but play games with the kids and so they weren't prepared for the upper grades. The downstairs thought the upstairs were too lazy to individualize their instruction to meet the needs of the kids. There was a lot of tension. (Follow-up interview with 3rd grade teacher)

In another school, the tension existed between the African American and Hispanic teachers. The former were upset at the districts' extra funding for bilingual education programs which they saw as benefiting the Latino children at the expense of African American children in their school. Racial strains between black and white faculty and/or parents were also present in many of these schools. In several buildings, there was hostility between the administrators (and their supporters) and a particular group of teachers. To overcome these antagonisms, it was necessary to initiate several conversations.

The first conversation typically focused on the moral purposes of school reform. One question we asked during our initial interviews was, "In what ways does your school help prepare students to live in a democratic society?" In several early discussions, we asked faculty to consider ways in which school reform might help their students break the cycle of poverty in their community. However, most of our references to the moral purpose of school reform focused on the lives of the students in their building. Early in and throughout our relationship, we encouraged faculty to put the existential quality of their students' lives in school at the center of our work. We have often suggested that although the faculty cannot do much, if anything, about the quality of their students' lives on the street or in their homes, they do have an opportunity to create a culture in the school that is safe for each child's body and emotions and one that honors, for example, the students' intellectual, communicative, kinesthetic, and artistic talents. Fortunately, this call to significantly improve the existential lives of their students in school seems to have resonated with all but the most cynical individuals. Most importantly, this "moral appeal" provided a strong rationale for working through conflicts in mutually respectful ways. In all the years of our work, only one school failed to respond positively to our request to put aside their acrimony for the sake of the students. As illustrated below, the power of this moral rational for reform work should not be underestimated.

> Baker Elementary has been plagued by bitter disputes along racial, gender, and hierarchical lines for several years, and we were asked by the superintendent to work with this school to avoid firing the principal and a subsequent public controversy. The principal has had many conflicts with teach-

ers who see him as dictatorial, disrespectful, and vindictive. The principal and the few teachers who support him view the teachers' concerns as an indication of racism, since his most vocal critics are White while he himself is Black. Due to this animosity, we asked members of the school community (during our initial interviews) if these conflicts had any impact on their students. Over and over again, the faculty said no. When we read numerous statements to the contrary from interviews we had with their students, the room went silent. Over and over we read statements that not only indicated the students' awareness of the faculty's conflicts, but also their anguish that these conflicts caused. Many teachers were shocked and surprised by the students' insights into how the conflicts hurt the school's reputation and their collective identity. Perhaps for the first time, the faculty realized the importance of working through their disagreements. (summary of field notes)

Contextualizing reform work in terms of students' existential experiences has been propitious in addressing the ways in which these schools have resolved or failed to resolve conflicts.

A long-standing problem emerged in our meeting today. Like many schools, teachers were assigned to monitor the halls prior to the start of the day. However, several teachers complained, "They [the students] get all juiced up and come to class ready to rock and roll, instead of ready to work." In response, one of the teachers who had this responsibility said that she has tried to keep the students from acting out, but that there are too many of them. It was noted that this situation has been a problem for several years. No one wanted to be the hall monitor. At this point, we asked what would be the best way to begin the school day *for the students*. One teacher shared her vision of children being welcomed into the school and into each classroom. Several said it should be a time for relaxed conversations and activities. After several more minutes of conversation, a proposal emerged that received consensus: Instead of having a floor monitor, all teachers would stand outside their doors fifteen minutes prior to the beginning of school, and personally welcome each child into their rooms. At the same time, the principal and other staff members would wander the halls welcoming students to school. In this way, each child would receive some personal attention as s/he entered his/her classroom. (summary of field notes)

Once a faculty member internalized this rationale (putting students' quality of life first), they seemed to be able to move beyond their acrimonious histories.

These additional conversations focused on the nature and dynamics of conflict in the reform process. As several of the school reformers mentioned, we suggested that faculty reconceptualize and embrace conflict as a natural and positive aspect of people working together for common purposes (i.e., the thoughtful education of children). Unfortunately, the lack or avoidance of conflict was often viewed as a desirable goal. However, without conflict there can rarely be growth. As we shared with the faculty at Baker Elementary School, "People of good will have legitimate differences, and differences always hold the potential for conflict. If we are afraid of conflict we will not be able to honestly explore or do what we need to do." At the same time, we stressed that the resolution of disagreements should not mean a victory by some faculty at the expense of others.

We also initiated conversations about rituals of personal interaction among the faculty. In nearly every school in which we worked, these interactions were often counterproductive:

> Due to the antagonisms among the faculty, it was necessary to discuss what we called "standards of interaction." That is, we initiated a discussion about how colleagues should communicate. Out of this discussion, the faculty reached consensus to: 1) never talk negatively about a colleague behind his or her back; 2) focus on the issue rather than the individual who expresses a contrary point of view; 3) instead of finding blame, focus on what needs to be done to correct or improve the situation; 4) avoid expressing hearsay information as if it came from direct experience; 5) speak only for oneself (e.g., avoid saying, "Several of us think . . ."); 6) listen carefully and understand what someone has said or done before responding or reacting; and 7) give gentle reminders to individuals who forget to follow these standards of interaction.[2] (summary of field notes)

Closely related to these standards of interaction, were useful discussions initiated for the purpose of giving and receiving feedback. These conversations often began with exploring times when faculty received or gave inappropriate feedback (e.g, receiving "put downs," irrelevant information, or embarrassing feedback in public). From deconstructing these autobiographies, we generated insights into what the faculty wanted to avoid. Next, these discussions usually focused on constructing a list of "feedback norms" similar to the ones at Columbus Elementary School.

> After a long discussion that began with sharing "feedback nightmares," followed by an analysis of these stories, the faculty reached consensus on the following feedback norms: 1) before giving negative feedback, be sure to identify something positive about a colleague's work; 2) give negative feedback in private; 3) whenever something worthwhile is noticed, be sure to tell the individual; 4) ask for permission before giving negative feedback; and 5) if inappropriate feedback is given, gently remind the individual of the previously agreed-upon feedback norms. (summary of field notes)

We found that accepting and learning how to address conflict in ways that promote rather than tear apart a school's sense of community was a crucial aspect of these reform efforts.

A final conversation related to conflict involved issues of jurisdiction. At the core of our efforts to create a more democratic culture within these schools, we encouraged them to carefully consider the principle of making certain that those who were most affected by a given decision have a direct voice in making that decision. This has led to conversations about who has the power to make what types of decisions. For example, decisions that directly effect only a given classroom would ideally be made by the teacher and his or her students. A decision that impacts only the lower grades should be made by those teachers who teach grades 1–3 (and, if appropriate, their students). At the same time, there are often decisions that, while not directly impacting one's colleagues, do have some effect upon them. For example, the lower-grade elementary teachers could make a decision that might have some impact on the teachers (and students) in higher grades or the school administrators. In these situations, it was necessary to discuss the importance of notifying these secondary stakeholders so they have an opportunity to discuss any concerns they might have about a particular decision. In a few schools, we helped sort out the question of jurisdiction by identifying potential "spheres of influence" in their school along with the primary and secondary stakeholders associated with each of these "spheres" in ways similar to those at Jason Elementary/Middle School (see p. 66, Table 4.1).

To summarize, our efforts to create a democratic culture for the purpose of substantively reforming the education of children in these schools focused primarily on three goals. As leaders of these projects, we redistributed power within a given school by establishing several democratic structures for making policy (e.g., creation of LTs and SGs), devised rituals for helping all school community members find their voices and hence experience a sense of efficacy (e.g., consensus decision making, seeking out those who are silent), and fostered communication patterns to help community members work through conflicts. We now turn our attention to the several struggles we confronted in helping these schools create a democratic foundation upon which they were able to develop a plan to thoughtfully and significantly improve the education of their children.

STRUGGLES AND DILEMMAS

Space does not allow for a full discussion of the numerous struggles we faced in our efforts to alter the culture of these schools. However, we found three aspects of this work to be particularly challenging and thus worth supplemental attention.

Victimization

Many educators view people who live in poverty as victims who are battered by their socioeconomic circumstances. As several scholars (Anyon, 1997; Bloom, 2004; Pakalov, 1993; Payne, 1995; Shannon, 1998) have illustrated, these children are routinely victimized in school. However, children are not the only victims in these schools. Perhaps more disturbing has been the expressions of victimization that emerged from school faculty. For example, Anyon (1997) notes that faculty often feel battered by poor administrative support, lack of sufficient funding, overcrowding, poor physical facilities, lack of parental involvement, students who are not well prepared and often

TABLE 4.1
Spheres of Influence

Spheres of Influence	Primary Stakeholders	Secondary Stakeholders	Realm of Decisions (examples of)
classroom	teachers	students, parents, program director, other teachers, principal	curriculum, instruction, students' learning, assessment, classroom rules, atmosphere, and layout
elementary program	program director, teachers, counselor, aides	principal, parents, students	coordinated projects, rituals, safety rules, graduation criteria, and hiring new faculty
secondary program	program director, teachers, counselors	principal, parents, students	same as above
academic departments	department chair, faculty	principal, program director, students	same as above
faculty assembly	five elected teachers/staff, principal, assistant principal, program directors	faculty, staff, students, parents	campus-wide policies (e.g., discretionary funds, grievance procedures, hiring criteria)
central administration	principal, assistant principal, program directors	central administration, faculty	building and grounds policies, administrative paper work, hiring new faculty, communication with central office, board of education, and state DOE, community relations

alienated, the public's perception that they are inadequate, and staff development that promises relief but rarely remains involved long enough to even know about, let alone seriously address, their problems. As one veteran teacher stated,

> Before Dr. Orlando [the superintendent], Ms. Black [the principal], and you guys came, this school was a mess. No one cared. I mean it, no one—not the principal, not the central administrators, not the parents, not the kids, not the Department of Education, no one. A lot of teachers would say, "If they don't care, why should I?" For years, this school was a pit. If you had a problem, there was no one to help. If you tried to do something worthwhile, everyone else would look at you like you were nuts. "What's the point?" they'd say. No one gave a damn, so why should you work your butt off for nothing? (Follow-up interview)

Although there are many obvious reasons why faculty in high-poverty schools are overwhelmed by external constraints and thus can be viewed as victims of their circumstances, we have found it necessary to challenge the perception of these limitations as excuses for complacency.

As the quote above suggests, the most devastating ramification of victimization is the sense of powerlessness that comes with it. Being a victim drastically undermines a faculty's sense of efficacy. As long as faculty view themselves as victims, as impotent people working against overwhelming forces, real school reform remains an illusion. As a result, one of our most important struggles was to help faculty alter this corrosive self-perception. Although we often agreed with their assessment of the difficulties of their occupation, we found it necessary to challenge their sense of powerlessness.

> I'd say the most important event came during the first year. Several teachers started to blame Daniel (the HEC consultant) for the tensions in the building that had been brought out into the open. Some suggested that what we were doing was a waste of time and that the only person benefitting was Daniel. I can't remember exactly what he said but it was something like, "Listen, you can blame me if you want, or the parents, central administrators, or kids. You can't change the type of children who come to this school, you can't change their parents, you can't change their neighborhoods, you can't change their histories, but you can ask me to leave. It's up to you. Only you can improve what really happens inside this school for the six hours children are here each day. Only you can make the education of your students more meaningful or not. Only you can change this school to be the school you want it to be. Think about what you want to do, and let me know if you still want to work with me when I return next week." He wasn't defensive or angry when he said that, and it really got us thinking. It was at that moment when we, or at least the majority of us, realized that if we weren't going to make this school better, no one was. (Follow-up interview with school Title I coordinator)

A common question asked of the faculty in these schools was, "If not you, who [will improve the education of these children], and if not now, when [will the education of these children improve]"? In addition to directly challenging their sense of victimization, we typically initiated conversations that explored their power, similar to that at Union Elementary School:

> The discussion with the faculty addressed spheres of power or what some scholars call "locus of control." We asked them to identify those types of decisions that they had control over, those they had influence over, and those they had, from their perspective, no influence over. At first, they felt they had no control over anything, but with a little prodding everyone realized that, at the least, they make decisions over much of what happens in their own classrooms, especially concerning how they respond to students' ideas, attitudes, and behavior. We did not contradict their perceptions of powerlessness, but rather asked them to focus on the work of their three study groups (e.g., School Climate/Culture, Curriculum/Instruction, and Community/ Parent Involvement) on two types of decisions. Namely, those realms of decisions that they clearly have control over, and those they can reasonably expect to have some influence over. By focusing on what they had control over and what they might reasonably be able to influence rather than what they couldn't do, their perception of their own power gradually increased throughout the year. Now there are very few issues they see outside of their sphere of influence. For example, in an effort to spend more time working together, they wrote a memo to the central administration asking if they could leave the district-wide workshop at noon on Martin Luther King's holiday to work together on their reform plan. What we found most impressive was their response to the administration's denial. Instead of blaming and complaining about being thwarted and thus victimized again, they merely turned their attention to finding another afternoon to meet. (summary of field notes)

Slowly, over time, the faculties in these schools began to question the limitations placed upon them by external agencies. Tentatively at first, and more boldly as the work continued, they answered the questions, if not you, who? if not now, when?, with the answer, us and now.

> The faculty at Highland Elementary School decided to eliminate, for the most part, phonics-centered language arts and traditional memory recall-based science and social studies lessons. In its place, they had developed 1) a process-based writing program that emphasizes fluency of expression and teaches mechanics as a process of copyediting, 2) integrated thematic units of study based upon the natural and social sciences, and 3) a literature-based reading program. However, several faculty expressed serious concerns about the school's scores on the state's competency test. An animated discussion ensued around this issue. Some teachers felt the proposed changes might be too drastic and if the students didn't perform well on the test, the school standing would be in jeopardy. Others thought it was worth the risk given

their previous discussions. Someone suggested we meet with the State's Department of Education's testing office to see what they thought before moving ahead. A meeting was set up, and to our surprise, the representatives enthusiastically supported this school's plan. One stated, "Our studies have indicated that children in literature-rich classrooms, where lots of writing occurs, do best on our test. Spelling, for example, is not really a spelling test. It's a word-recognition test. Children who read and write a lot do better on this test than those who merely memorize spelling words. Kids who are asked to make what they read meaningful score much better on the comprehension test than those who have been taught to identify the 'main idea or character' of a paragraph or story." (summary of field notes)

Ultimately, faculty were encouraged and supported to develop a sense of existential freedom as discussed in Sartre's (1956) *Being and Nothingness.* While they were "born" into a world not of their own making and thus were not free to do whatever they wanted, they were free to determine *their experience* of this world. As teachers working in high poverty schools, they faced many substantive constraints. They could view impediments as absolute limits to complain about, as excuses for not being more proactive, as examples of why nothing ever changes, as reasons for their cynicism, or as challenges toward which they can apply their creativity, moral courage, and determination. While we encouraged faculty to adopt the latter of these dispositions, this type of change could not be simply mandated. It took significant time and only really began to change once a given faculty honestly experienced the expansion of their sphere of influence. In schools that went through this transformation, we noted that faculty took greater responsibility for the way in which they lived their occupational lives.

Since this was the first Leadership Team meeting of the year (third year of our partnership), we asked each member to share their reflections from the summer break. One teacher said something especially noteworthy: "I went to a workshop on thematic curriculum, and after the overview of the process we were put into groups to work on the development of a thematic unit. Our group spent the first fifteen minutes complaining about how the speaker's ideas wouldn't work in their school because of whatever. Finally, I told them to stop complaining and just start working. All that bellyaching really brought me back to our first year, and all the excuses we used to make as to why we couldn't do this or that." Another teacher then stated, "The same thing happened to me. I went to a workshop on discipline, we also broke up into groups, and my group started off just complaining how this wouldn't work and that wouldn't work, and I was the one who finally stopped them. I said, 'Let's get on with it.' All that wasted energy." (summary of field notes)

Assuming this existential responsibility helped faculty avoid getting distracted by the countless ordeals they faced as teachers in urban settings. Most importantly, developing this existential responsibility often provided faculty with more power than previously thought possible. It seemed that teachers first had to experience having significant influence over their own occupational lives before they were able help their students and families break the oppressive cycle of intergenerational poverty. Without these experiences, it was very difficult for them to design a learning community in their classrooms that could, in turn, prepare young people to meaningfully influence the circumstances of their own lives. Although gratified by the many faculty who altered the way in which they came to view their occupational positionality, addressing the issue of victimization remained a major struggle in our work.

Leadership

As previously mentioned, initially we assumed the primary role of leadership for the purposes of facilitating these school-based reform projects. Given this position, we have been confronted with two concerns related to leadership in these schools.

First, as previously noted, the creation of a LT and SGs resulted in a redistribution of power, and we found it necessary to address the ramifications of this reallocation when noticed by building administrators. While several of the principals appreciated the broadening of power within their buildings, many others had difficulty adjusting to their new status:

> The principal shared that he was confused and somewhat "lost." He didn't know if he was really needed anymore now that the LT had taken over so much of the running of the school. In response, we first reviewed why he felt this way. It was true that many of his former responsibilities were now shared among his faculty, but that might not be the real cause of his "extra time." We reminded him that most of his time prior to these reforms was spent in "crisis management" which now needed little of his attention. We recalled the special role he played on the LT for initiating and supporting the reform efforts. Although our comments of support seemed to ease his concerns, we realized that we haven't given enough thought to helping building administrators make this transition. We agreed to continue our discussion during our next visit. (summary of field notes)

As our previous discussion of Jane, the principal of Bradley Elementary School (see chapter 3), illustrates, some principals come to view our participation as infringing upon their domain. In any case, asking principals to adjust their leadership role was difficult, especially due to past animosities that existed in many of the buildings. For example, in one school (in a correctional facility) we were asked to leave specifically due to our efforts at redistributing power among the faculty:

> The principal told us he did not like the way "things" were going, and our services were terminated. We are not surprised by his decision. The hierarchy of this school is deeply entrenched and long standing. There is little

respect between the faculty and administration. We remembered that during our debriefing meeting with the principal and superintendent following the first meeting with the faculty, the principal said he agreed with everything we said except when we told the faculty that they would determine what reforms to make in the school; that no policies would be imposed upon them as a result of our work. We remembered him telling us that the faculty needed to change their values and practices. Our response was to point out that while the teachers needed to change, it would not occur through imposition from superordinates, but only through meaningful discourse. Nevertheless, from the beginning, the principal was uncomfortable with the power being distributed to the faculty. (summary of field notes)

In the years we were involved in these projects, this was the only time we were asked to terminate our participation prior to the end of the planning year. Nevertheless, as external change agents, we did not devote enough attention to the ramifications of this work for building administrators. As Talbot and Crow (1998) pointed out, the transition from conventional to a democratic principal can be rough on one's occupational perception, and clearly, more can be done to make this conversion smoother.

The second leadership issue that needed more attention in our work concerned the problem of transferring leadership from ourselves to the school community. While we assumed the authority necessary to initiate and maintain these projects, one of our struggles was to eventually withdraw, leaving behind a culture that could sustain ongoing, substantive educational discourse and decision making. Thus, identifying and transferring leadership to individuals who would and could make faculty conversations and decision making an integral facet of occupational life in these schools became one of the most important and difficult aspects of our work. If we could not facilitate this relocation of leadership in a given school, then we did not fully realize our ultimate goal: the establishment of a democratic-minded learning community within each school.

In those schools that had dynamic, thoughtful, and communicative principals, the transfer of power was relatively smooth and easy. However, while most principals were adequate managerial leaders, they often did not have the talent necessary for transformative leadership. In addition, many principals were highly mobile, never staying in one building for more than a few years. As a result, it has been reassuring to note that most of the schools maintained their LT and transformed their SGs into standing committees for the purpose of promoting school discourse and decision making beyond the initial planning year. In these schools, many issues were directed to the LT instead of the building administrators. The work of Norris Elementary School's LT was similar to other schools that permanently modified their governance structure:

The next agenda item was a proposal to stop the practice of selling candy to children. The LT reviewed several concerns, such as the physical and dental health of the children, the negative effect (hyperactivity) that sugar has on several of the children, and the ethical dilemma of making it easy for children who do not have much money to spend it on candy. At this point, a representative from the kitchen staff raised a financial concern. She noted that selling candy has been a practice for many years at the school, and had become an important supplement to the low wages of the women who work in the kitchen. After a lengthy discussion, the LT agreed to support a proposal to allow candy to be sold only to those students who have parental permission, limit the amount of candy each child can buy, and revisit the issue in two months to assess its impact. (summary of field notes)

The previously discussed democratic structures and rituals were particularly valuable in those schools in which the principal left the building prior to the completion of the reform project.

At the LT meeting today we noticed that once again, Ms. White, the new principal, was not present. However, we were impressed that after two months into their second year of the project, this LT and thus the school was operating effectively. We left the meeting and found Ms. White in her office. In our conversation, she shared her feelings of "not being needed" and "out of the loop." She wondered if this school really needed a principal, and thought her presence might be resented. We encouraged her to get involved in spite of these feelings and told her we would help her move into the flow of events. We emphasized the crucial role the principal plays in times of substantive change. After discussing her situation, she agreed to become more involved. We then went back into the LT meeting and discussed ways to bring the principal into the process. Several teachers empathized with Ms. White, and others apologized if their actions implied that she wasn't needed. The meeting ended with two members of the LT agreeing to "bring her up to speed." (summary of field notes)

This structure served as a foundation upon which schools continued their ongoing reform work.

At today's meeting, the Curriculum Committee discussed the progress of the school's goal to use more inquiry-based pedagogy. Specifically, we discussed their stated strategy to develop a science curriculum that would include at least one "hands on" experiment each week. After a few minutes of discussion, it was clear that little had been accomplished. Only a few teachers had by this time (end of October) implemented this strategy. After several people speculated on the causes for this failure (e.g., no time, concern over the state's standardized test, lack of science knowledge, fear of failure), the committee members decided to identify and interview the teachers who were implementing this goal to find out what they are doing. The committee then decided to publicize this information so that others will have some ideas of how to start. Finally, it was decided that the primary agenda item for the next meeting would be to review the results from their interviews. In the meantime, a few members volunteered to explore staff-development resources to help the faculty meet this goal. (summary of field notes)

Establishing democratic structures made the transference of power possible, but it did not, by itself, promote the ongoing reflection and action we hoped would emerge from our work. It was also necessary to locate those individuals in each school who were willing to assume responsibility for continuing the reform discourses.

Fortunately, once LTs and SGs were firmly established beyond the initial planning year, this structure allowed for individuals who had leadership talents to manifest them regardless of their official position in their school. As Quantz and his colleagues (1991, p. 104) have stated,

> Transformative leadership theory, however, must argue that leaders can and should be located at all levels of an organization, for transformative leadership achieves its power and authority not through domination but through democracy and emancipation. And democracy requires individuals at all levels to assume responsibility for constructing a democratic community. Leadership theory must back away from the assumption that the administrators are the only leaders in the school and must focus on how leadership is to be fostered at all levels of a school.

Although we provided leadership during the planning year, as the work continued, we took note of those teachers, parents, support staff, and of course, building administrators that assumed leadership:

> During our debriefing session today, we tried to identify school and community leadership potential for the future. In particular, we discussed Ms. Bove, the school counselor, and Ms. Jackson, a fifth grade teacher, who had the respect of their colleagues, who were honest, who could speak in public forums, and who were committed to the project. We made plans to nurture their leadership potential. (summary of field notes)

During our work in these schools, we identified and supported classroom teachers, school counselors, parents, Title I coordinators, and in one case, a substitute teacher as "unofficial" school leaders. Increasing the leadership capacity of a school required us to look well beyond the official position individuals had, and to nurture the leadership talents in whoever possessed them within a given building.

To summarize, all too often, reform efforts die once "the leader" leaves the building. As a result, establishing a structure that encourages participation of the entire school community is crucial for any serious effort to promote ongoing school-based reform discourse. However, these structures were not enough. We also had to consciously identify and support those individuals in a given school who seemed to possess qualities of "transformational leadership," that is, people who had vision, the respect and admiration of their colleagues, a commitment to participatory democracy, talent for facilitating their colleagues' work, and an optimistic work ethic (Quantz et. al., 1991; Yukl, 1994). Unfortunately, our ability to locate and support these individuals was only partially successful. It remained an aspect of our work that demanded more than we could give to most of these schools. It continues to be an area of concern that we, reformers and scholars, need to pay more attention to in the future.

Authenticity

As several scholars have noted (e.g., Anderson and Grinberg, 1998; Barker, 1993; Beare, 1993; Campbell and Southworth, 1990; Chapman and Boyd, 1986; Gitlin and Margonis, 1995; Hargreaves, 1994; Lipman, 1997; Smyth, 1993), discourses located in many school-based reform projects are often inauthentic:

> Shared governance structures may not result in significant participation in decisions but, instead, result in contrived collegiality, reinforced privilege, and even create a tighter iron cage of control for participants. . . . From the grassroots level, teachers in schools are increasingly complaining that participation is often bogus, takes time from their interactions with students, and intensifies an already heavy workload leading in many cases to teacher burnout. (Anderson, 1998, p. 572)

Anderson goes on to suggest that, "In many cases, attempts at increased participation are sincere but poorly conceived and implemented or caught up in a larger institutional and societal logic that is antithetical to norms of participation" (1998, p. 586). In response, several scholars have tried to identify what they consider to be the characteristics of authentic collaborative work among school communities.

Hargreaves (1994, pp. 192–93) suggests that bona fide, collaborative cultures tend to be spontaneous as opposed to administratively regulated, voluntary rather than compulsory, development oriented rather than implementation oriented, pervasive across time and space instead of fixed in time and space, and unpredictable rather than predictable. Anderson (1998, pp. 586–595) identifies democracy and equity, broad inclusiveness of school community members, few restrictions on what topics are open for school-based decision making, open communication without regard to position within the school, and contested relationships with external powers as elements in genuine participatory, school-based reform.

We agree with the sentiments expressed by these scholars. Without authenticity, school-based reforms are a sham, and thus not worthy of our time and energy, or the time and energy of the school communities in which we have worked. Perhaps the most important goal of our work was to provide a context in which the school community could authentically discuss the education of their children. Although discussion of authenticity has been instructive and comprehensive, we have, in light of our work, a few additional comments to make regarding this extremely important aspect of school-based reform.

Given these previously mentioned characteristics, our work in these schools seemed to be both authentic and inauthentic depending upon the individuals involved, the topics and perceived progress of our discourses, and the timing of these discourses. For example, several of these reform projects were initiated by the district administration. At times, these projects were started against the expressed wishes of the school's faculty. As such, our work in these locations clearly began as inauthentic projects. One might conclude that anything we might have done, therefore, was inappropriate especially given our commitment to the previously discussed democratic principles. However, we have drawn a different conclusion, namely, that authenticity has less to do with the manner in which particular projects might get initiated and developed, and more to do with the willingness to openly address the way in which members of a school community existentially experience the process of reform at any given time.

> Our very first conversation with the faculty focused on their request [which was denied by the district administration] *not* to participate in this school-based reform project. We asked them to share with us why they did not want to participate. Many noted the long history of the central administration's desire to "micromanage" what happens in schools. In addition, concerns were raised about the time needed to participate, the potential additional work, the discomfort of working through conflicts, fear of the unknown, and skepticism regarding who would make final decisions. After each of these concerns were addressed, we challenged the faculty [in a very warm and friendly way] to think of ways in which this work could be meaningful in spite of the administration's "directive" as the primary focus of our next meeting. (summary of field notes)

Several schools entered into these reform projects with the expectation that it would be no different and no more authentic than any other "staff development" programs in which they were required to participate. Ironically, these difficult beginnings did not taint the entire process. To the contrary, they often created an opportunity to develop authentic trust and communication.

Another aspect of this discourse concerns the implication that, in order to be authentic, individuals must feel free to openly express themselves during discussions. Although this is an extremely worthwhile situation, we have come to believe that authenticity has less to do with verbal expression and more to do with the reasons behind one's decision to participate in a given interchange:

> Today, we discussed Gloria Ladson-Billings's book, *The Dreamkeepers*. Given that 98 percent of the students and 50 percent of the faculty are of African American heritage, we thought this book would engage the faculty. However, this was not the case. Even before the discussion, Ellen, a black teacher, told us she hated the book. When we asked her why, she said it was filled with nonsense, but wouldn't elaborate. During the discussion she seemed not

to be listening. The teachers who did speak endorsed Ladson-Billings's central thesis, and when we consciously tried to generate more diverse reactions, we were confronted with silence. Despite numerous efforts to solicit the faculty's reactions, this conversation did not generate a diversity of responses. Afterwards, we asked some teachers why they didn't participate. Most avoided the question, but Julie, a novice African American teacher, said she was inspired but also angered by the book because she saw many examples of teaching in this school that were not "culturally responsive." She didn't speak during the discussion because she didn't want to offend her colleagues by expressing this thought. (summary of field notes)

What does this conversation tell us about authenticity? Was Ellen's refusal to speak publicly about her negative reaction to this book inauthentic? If her silence was because she hadn't read the book, and/or was alienated from the project as a whole, then her initial criticism and subsequent silence might be an example of inauthentic involvement. If Ladson-Billings's descriptions of "culturally relevant teaching" were too contrary to the way she taught and thus the subject matter personally threatening, then her silence might have been an effort to avoid being put on the defensive. In this latter case, our failure, as facilitators of this discussion, to critique rather than merely neutrally present Ladson-Billings's ideas might have contributed to an inauthentic situation for Ellen. On the other hand, it is important to remember that Ellen's level of authenticity was ultimately her own decision. As Sartre (1956, pp. 47–70) notes in his discussion of this issue (which he refers to as "bad-faith"), Ellen might merely have made a decision to "go through the motions" of being a teacher. If so, our facilitation of this discussion would probably have not made a difference to her.

Certainly, some of the teachers in this discussion were not authentic participants. However, to say that Julie was inauthentic would be problematic from our perspective. Perhaps her silence was not a sign of spuriousness, but one of self-protection due to her lack of seniority (despite our efforts to make these conversations safe); perhaps it was her inability at that moment to express herself without being angry and thus embarrassed; or perhaps it was because she was sensitive to her colleagues' feelings of defensiveness and recognized that forcing this issue would be counter-productive at this particular time. Regardless of her reasons, her silence did not represent a lack of authenticity nor genuine engagement. In this discussion she was an authentic participant who was engaged in an active, however, internal dialogue. It is important not to equate public verbosity with authenticity. No matter how carefully a school reform project might manifest the previously mentioned characteristics, each individual decides for him or herself whether or not to participate authentically.

Finally, it is important to note, as Buber (1958) did in *I and Thou*, the role that reciprocity plays in questions of authenticity. It has been our experience that authenticity attracts itself. People who approach life (in this case, occupational life) in an authentic manner, seem to gravitate to others who also are living authentically. As a result, the issue of authenticity, from a change agent's perspective, was largely a matter of self-authenticity. By focusing on being authentic ourselves, rather than playing the role of "change agent," we connected with those members of a given school community who were also interested in working authentically to improve the education of their children.

However, what about those individuals who resisted authentic engagement in these projects? Do we ignore these individuals, marginalize them, and hope they leave for another school, or pretend that they are participating when they are only "going through the motions?" Clearly, it is useless to try and convince someone to become authentically involved if they do not want to be. As previously mentioned, one of the characteristics of authentic participation is its voluntary quality. However, initially we required faculty to attend regular school reform meetings that were negotiated as part of their "work day," but made it clear that no one was required to volunteer their time:

> Exactly at 4:15, two teachers who had been sitting by the windows got up and walked across the entire library during the middle of a conversation and left the building. Since the meeting was only half over, it was a clear statement of resistance. These teachers had expressed their lack of enthusiasm at the first faculty meeting in which we determined when and how often the faculty would participate. At that time we expressed the importance of having everyone at these meetings so that no one felt marginalized by the final decisions. However, the teachers' contract limited meetings to one rather than the two hours needed. As a result, we agreed that anyone who wanted to leave these meetings could do so, and this bold walk across the library was a clear indication of these teachers' unwillingness to participate in what they saw as "just another program." (summary of field notes)

After approximately six weeks, in which we consciously sought their input on a variety of topics, these teachers began to participate authentically in these and study group meetings. Developing honest relationships with individuals who are initially suspicious of any change efforts was one of our most important, creative challenges. As one fifth grade teacher told us,

> At first I refused to participate. I made it clear to everyone that I wanted nothing to do with this whole business. In response, they [the rest of the school] allowed me to supervise students in the building [along with community volunteers] while the faculty met [each Wednesday afternoon]. What I really appreciated was the perception that my helping the volunteers was a *real* contribution. No one looked at my withdrawal as a put down to me or the reform. Eventually, I was drawn into it, mostly because Daniel kept at me, and showed me how my involvement was needed. (Follow-up interview)

The importance of generating authenticity through reciprocity is an often overlooked and yet crucial aspect in understanding this phenomenon. Perhaps the most crucial implications are that being authentic is more important than expecting others to be authentic, and that questions of authenticity need to be openly and honestly addressed wherever and whenever they arise during these projects.

REFLECTIONS OF CHAPTER 4: MICROPOLITICS OF SCHOOL REFORM

This chapter described the ways in which we, as external change agents, worked with various educational communities in their effort to transform the organizational culture of their schools for the purpose of substantively improving the education of their students. These efforts included the establishment of democratic rituals and structures, expanding the voices of all school community members, and addressing conflict that is found within a given building. In addition, we discussed issues of victimization, leadership, and authenticity with which we struggled. However, there are a few additional issues that educational leaders and scholars might find useful, and are thus addressed.

The first issue concerns the place of pedagogy in these reform projects. Specifically, some time ago, at a meeting of "educational reformers," our approach to school-based reform was criticized by an individual who questioned our initial emphasis on governance rather than pedagogy. Although discourses about the education of children are central to our work (see chapter 5), the criticism was well deserved. Within a few years of working as external change agents, we soon realized that until a school community can work together as genuine colleagues, discussions of pedagogy are of little value. Until a school community is able to make important decisions, pedagogical talk remains just that—talk. Fullan (1993) is correct in his observations that changing the substance of education depends upon creating an organizational culture that fosters faculty ownership over and commitment to whatever changes are made through honest, open, and comprehensive dialogue. As Yankelovich (1999) notes and as we have observed, dialogue (rather than debates or disputes) in which people come together as equals, and who listen with empathy and seek to understand each other, and who are willing to examine assumptions and ideas without judging their own or others' self-worth, can transform the nature of one's occupational situation from one of conflict, mistrust, and isolation to one of community and collaboration. Only after a school community is able to develop such communicative patterns of interaction, can pedagogical talk become transformed into actual changes in what children learn, the way in which they learn, and the climate in which they learn. For those reformers, who like us, place liberal, critical, and social democracy at the center of children's education (see chapter 1), it soon becomes apparent that unless faculty learn to work with each other toward these goals, they will rarely do so with the students in their classrooms. Educational leaders involved in school-based reform projects make a mistake if they ignore what on the surface might seem as "procedural" or "decision-making protocols," in favor of delving directly into issues of pedagogy. It is important to remember that school-based reform discourses are significantly different from graduate seminars. While the latter need not strive for consensus or directly result in the alterations of specific children's schooling, the former must be focused and lead to definite decisions that the school community supports.

Second, it is important to briefly address the relationship between democracy and values of social justice and equity. Some might well argue that developing more democratic structures, rituals, and values in a school does not guarantee the promotion of a more socially just and equitable school or society. Might not a school that creates a democratic ethos and structure for adults have the option to create an unjust and demeaning educational experience for students and thus perpetuate the inequities currently found in the United States? Finally, if the answer to the above question is "yes" (and we believe it is), then what if any, responsibility do democratic-minded external change agents have in this situation?

Space does not allow for an adequate discussion; however, a few comments in response to this concern are necessary. Our commitment to democracy is not rooted in idealist essentialism. Rather, it is deeply connected to Dewey's (1920) pragmatism. As Rorty (1989) suggests, the primary value of democracy lies in its ability to resolve conflicts and make decisions in ways that minimize cruelty among those who are members of a given community. It does not guarantee any particular sort of outcome or type of decision. Nevertheless, we noticed that adults in school-based reform projects drew meaningful connections to their work as a result of their participation in democratic discourse. For example, in each school, teachers were encouraged, and many opted, to establish democratic conversations with students (i.e., "town meetings") about their classroom experiences on a regular basis. As teachers began to internalize the "standards of interaction" or "norms for giving feedback" in their work with each other, they indicated how these communication patterns transformed their work with students. Similarly, as issues of racism, patriarchy, poverty, and other forms of marginalization were discussed in study groups and faculty retreats, several teachers expressed greater sensitivity to these issues in relation to their students and their families. Democracy provides the potential for a reduction in cruelty and humiliation within a given community, but provides no warranties.

As will be discussed in chapter 6, our responsibility as external change agents is not to impose decisions upon a school, but to provide space for open discourse and deliberation. On the other hand, we did not mute ourselves, but assumed responsibility for expressing our own ideas and values. However, in the end, it was the school community that had to make all final decisions. Although imposing change might alter school or societal structures, it also distorts human intelligence and empathy. As Dewey (1946, p. 139) insightfully noted,

> Doctrines, whether proceeding from Mussolini or Marx, which assume that because certain ends are desirable therefore those ends and nothing else will result from the use of force to attain them is but another example of the limitations put on intelligence by any absolutist theory. In the degree in which mere force is resorted to, actual consequences are themselves so compromised that the ends originally in view have in fact to be worked out afterwards by the method of experimental intelligence.

He goes on to argue that it is only through democratic, inclusive discourses that a given community (e.g., a school or society) can genuinely become more socially just and humane. To critique democracy for failing to rectify social injustice in the short run is to miss the point. Although we, as educational leaders of school-based reform projects, have often been disappointed with many of the specific goals or strategies that a given school adopted as a result of these reform projects, our optimism remains in tact as long as a given school community continues its commitment to study, discuss, and utilize democracy as a means to develop and grow.

Nevertheless, as previously mentioned, eventually these projects must address the education of children. After all, building a school's autonomy and establishing democratic structures, rituals, and values within its walls was not the central purpose of our involvement in these school-based reform efforts. In the next chapter, we explore the substance of what emerged from the deliberations that emerged within the democratic context we helped to create.

CHAPTER 5

Addressing the Conservative Agenda: Discourses of School-Based Reform

As discussed in the first chapter, the United States finds itself in the grip of a conservative restoration. Within the educational realm of society, this shift to the right has resulted in several initiatives such as efforts to privatize education through vouchers, to utilize standardized testing as the only tool for the assessment of children's learning and subsequent graduation or grade-level promotion, to make the results of such tests public and to equate the quality of a school's educational program and quality of teaching based upon the scores children receive on these tests, and to penalize those schools that fail to improve the test scores of their students, among other things. As discussed in chapter 1, this agenda has emerged from the economic and political realms of society and has been pushed by a variety of classes including the bourgeoisie, the intelligentsia, evangelical Christians, and Euro-American males. However, from the "ground floor" perspective, critiques of the conservative agenda seem terribly abstract and far removed from the challenges of educating children. To most school communities, it makes little difference what realm of society (e.g., government, business) or what class of people are pushing this conservative agenda. Public schools in the United States naturally respond to the concerns of societal forces that exist far beyond their immediate clients (i.e., children and parents). What is crucially important is how a school community responds to particular external pressures, whatever the agenda. In addition, if this conservative agenda is presented to educators as an architectonic force, then it is likely that school-reform conversations would soon degenerate into discourses of despair. What can an individual teacher or even an entire school do about the cultural shift to the right if it is presented as a grand ideological "glacier" moving across the globe? Presenting the challenges facing schools within this broad ideological context leads most educators to conclusions of powerlessness. Furthermore, even if one is successful in convincing a school community that right-wing politics and economics are the source of the misguided educational agenda being foisted upon them, their time is still best spent addressing the specific issues of educating their students, rather than on abstract, ideologies.

*Thanks to Daniel Baron and Carol Myers for their assistance with this chapter.

Nevertheless, the inclination of our society to embrace this conservative ideology and to reform schools in light of its principles is indeed troubling, and requires serious deliberation beyond the walls of academia. The challenge before us is to initiate and facilitate these conversations in ways that school communities find authentic, relevant, and meaningful. As previously mentioned, the purpose of this particular chapter is to present a portrayal of discourses we have had with school communities as issues related to this renewed conservativism have arisen in the context of school-based reform projects. This portrayal is by no means exhaustive; nor are we suggesting that our response is the most productive of all possibilities. Rather, our goal is to articulate potentiality and invite an interchange of ideas among progressive-thinking educators in the hope that we may all benefit and emerge with a more compelling response to the very powerful conservative educational agenda that has emerged in our society.

ADDRESSING THE AGENDA

We begin our presentation with a caveat. As previously mentioned, discourses that occur in school communities with teachers, administrators, parents, support staff, and when appropriate, students, should not be confused with doctoral seminars (Habermas, 1975). In the latter, students and the professor read, discuss texts and personal experiences, and often speculate on the causes and ramifications of particular social and educational phenomena—all organized around a central topic. In addition, these discourses often introduce or utilize particular theoretical or conceptual schools of thought as a focus of study or as a lens through which the seminar explores ideas, structures, or activities of schooling. The purpose of doctoral seminars is to encourage scholarly inquiry. The nature of school-based reform discourse has a different purpose, namely, the generation of potential responses to specific ideas and events related to the responsibility of educating children. Given the workload of public educators, there is little tolerance for the type of abstract interchange typical of doctoral seminars in U.S. academic institutions. The creative challenge of these conversations is to make them both substantive and practical. That is, to make them conversations that focus on "what can be done" in ways that are intellectually rich and that avoid the utilitarianism often associated with conventional "staff development" programs. Although space does not allow for a complete rendition of the conversations we have had with school communities during the twelve years of work that was the basis for this book, what follows is a sampling of the topics and ideas that have emerged from efforts to address the conservative agenda now forcing its way upon our schools.

The Privatization of Schooling

Certainly one of the main ideas that has emerged from this conservative agenda is the idea that our children would be better off served by private rather than public schools (Chubb and Moe, 1990). In the vast majority of the schools in which we have worked, this effort to privatize schooling has not been an issue. From the perspective of these schools, there are far more pressing issues to discuss than the various "voucher" experiments that are currently occurring in the United States. However, we did have one experience with a school in Florida that was the victim of a voucher experiment meant to intimidate and punish schools in which children's scores on the state's competency exam continually fell below the minimum.

> The agenda for our first meeting with this school was interrupted because they just were told this morning that their students' test scores were once again, below the minimum and now their school would be publicly designated as a "failure." Faculty morale was completely shattered. During the last year they focused their entire curriculum and instruction on the content of this exam, but still they failed. Being identified as a failure, students would now have the opportunity to obtain a voucher equal to the amount that has been given to the school to educate each student. If students take this opportunity, the school as a whole will suffer. Naturally, the faculty feels ripped off. They do not think the state takes into consideration the difficulty this school has, given that many students transfer in and out of the building each year, parents who are often uninvolved in their children's education, and the few "promising" students who will now probably leave and go to a private school. There is tremendous trepidation and many questions among the faculty. What will happen to the students who stay behind? Will most of the faculty try to leave the building? For the teachers who stay, how will they deal with the stigma of being labeled a "failure"? (summary of field notes)

Unfortunately, due to scheduling difficulties, we were not able to pursue a relationship with this school. However, even this one conversation illustrated the potential negative impact the privatization of schooling can have on a specific school community. In most states, teachers have fought back through union lobbying activities in their state legislatures. However, with the Bush administration pushing a program initiated in his brother's state of Florida, union resistance has been sorely tested.

Although the privatization of schooling is disturbing, there are two aspects of this agenda that we find appealing. One of the central ideas of privatization is that schools should have relative autonomy from the state and be more responsive to the parents of their students. These are goals that we pursued in all of the schools where we worked (see chapters 3 and 4). In particular, we struggled to create what we like to call "school communities." Although the most important members of this community are teachers and their students, it also includes parents, administrators, and other interested local community members. Reaching out to parents took on a special role in our work:

> Today we discussed why so few parents are involved in the schooling of their children. Several ideas emerged from this discussion including the statement that most of the parents are members of the "working poor," who have little education themselves and often failed in school. Several teachers suggested that parents "don't care as much as former generations." Another teacher stated that many of the parents were "young, and didn't really know how to parent." However, one insightful teacher said, "Most parents in this community are intimidated by the school. They often didn't do well in school when they were children and so have lots of bad memories associated with it. Every time they come into the building, it brings up the humiliation of their own failures. If their child isn't doing well, they often blame themselves, and thus don't get involved because they feel ashamed. It's really a difficult problem." Toward the end of the discussion it seemed as if the faculty knew little about the actual parents in their community. A decision was made to take one day each month to visit the parents in their homes. The teachers would be given addresses of parents from different classrooms, knock on their doors, and if at home, ask the parents what they liked and didn't like about the school, and ask for suggestions of how the school could get more parents and other adults from the community (most of whom lived in a nearby trailer court) involved in the education of their children. After the first day out, the teachers came back excited and amazed by what they found out. Despite the poor reputation of the school, the parents actually were genuine supporters and indicated a strong desire to help out in any way they could. Many gave specific suggestions to get more adults involved. Many teachers who had been resistant, now looked forward to going out into the community next month. (summary of field notes)

Broadening a school's conception of itself as a community rather than just a building in which students go each morning, was a central focus of our work, and for good reason.

It is extremely difficult for any individual, acting alone, to "talk back" to the conservative educational agenda now facing schools. However, once a school finds its voice, it is in a much better position to respond effectively to these external powers:

> Today the Leadership Team (LT) discussed the implications of the "directive" that came from the new superintendent. For three years now we have worked with seven of this district's "high poverty" schools. In each, we have helped them develop a sense of unique identity and expanded their perceived locus of control. However, now these schools are probably facing their biggest challenge. The new superintendent has made several public announcements that her primary goal is to "ensure" that *every* [her emphasis] child is receiving a quality education, and that the way to do this is to have every child do and learn the exact same thing in every school in the district. In fact, she said that she believed every child in a given grade should be on the same page of the same book in each class and school no matter what school she or he is in. She added that this will also help solve the problems

associated with children moving from one school in the district to another. This goal, of course, directly challenges what we have been doing in this school for the last two years, namely, creating a unique educational program designed specifically for the students of this particular school. At this point, the LT is deeply committed to resisting the imposition of the district-wide curriculum and time schedule being proposed by the new superintendent. The discussion today focused on generating various strategies to respond to this central administrative initiative. Some of these included: obtaining a waiver due to the requirements of the Clinton administration's guidelines for Title I (anti-poverty educational funding) School-Based Initiative, which emphasizes school autonomy; exploring in more depth the ways in which the superintendent's proposal can be covertly circumvented if it becomes policy; notifying parents that the educational program that the school has established during the past two years is in jeopardy due to this proposal; scheduling a visit from the superintendent to the school to "show us off" and discuss her proposal in light of the school's current successes; and contacting the union to explore the contract and to see if this document can be used as a point of resistance. (summary of field notes)

Perhaps the most important aspect of our work has been to help schools become a community of educators who are bound to each other in a common cause, who develop a collective identity as a unique place of learning, and who eventually learn to speak and act in relative solidarity. As we will discuss below, the conservative agenda facing educators in our society is very powerful, and it is crucial for educators to respond, not as isolates, but as an authentic community.

Teaching for the Marketplace

One of the most successful victories of this conservative agenda is its casting of education within a marketplace rationale. Beginning with the *Nation at Risk* and continuing throughout both Republican and Democratic administrations, this view of schooling for the purpose of preparing children for work is taken for granted by nearly everyone in our society. Of course, it is important to remember that this orientation toward schooling has a long history in our society. Job preparation was the primary rationale for the creation of public schools during the first decades of the twentieth century (Bobbitt, 1924; Charters, 1924; Cubberley, 1916).

This rationale for schooling is especially strong in the high-poverty schools in which we have worked. Often it was the most dedicated and ardent advocates for the welfare of these children who were the most vocal in their support of this orientation. After all, except for a minuscule number of athletically and artistically intelligent children from these neighborhoods, education is perhaps their best option for escaping poverty. Ironically, the success of progressive politics during the second half of this century has made this argument even stronger. Prior to World War II, education did not provide this option, even where it was available (although often inadequate) to marginalized children. Even if a child born into oppressive conditions was successful in school, she or he would still be unlikely to gain entrance to economic, political, educational, or media institutions of society due to racism, sexism, classism, or other forms of discrimination. Although these social evils still exist in our society, the labor movement, the GI Bill, Civil Rights and Black Power movements, the Women's movement, the Physically Impaired movement, and the Ethnic Rights movements have had significant victories in their efforts to gain access to the previously mentioned institutions, and thus obtain a relatively prosperous standard of living. If children who live in poverty are "successful" in schools today, that is, if they internalize the current cultural capital, their chances of escaping poverty are much better now than during the first half of the twentieth century.

Unfortunately, the response to schooling-for-the-market from progressive educators and especially scholars has been ineffective in both public and educational realms of society. Most common, this response has been to call attention to its overwhelming power and the negative consequences of orientating education toward a business agenda. Too often we have failed to admit that a legitimate purpose of schooling is economic. All cultures, whether they have hunting-gathering, agricultural, industrial, technological, feudal, capitalist, or communist economies, have a responsibility to educate their children for the occupational realities of their society.

In responding to this market-driven educational rational for schooling, we have found it advantageous not to deny the importance of preparing children for future economic realities. Rather, we have engaged school communities in thoughtful discussions about the nature of this economic purpose for schooling:

> The next topic for today's retreat focused on schooling for work. In our initial interviews with the faculty, many responded to the question, "In what way(s) does your school help prepare students to live in a democratic society?" by references of keeping them off welfare once they become adults. When asked, retreat participants suggested that getting a job was clearly the most important reason for children going to school. At this point, we asked if they knew what jobs these children were being prepared for. We pointed out that the vast majority of jobs in our current market did not exist 100 years ago, and that the speed of economic change had accelerated greatly during our lifetimes. In exploring the implications of this statement, the faculty soon realized that the best preparation for work was to give students opportunities to be creative, critical (analytical), and cooperative since it was impossible to know what types of work will be required in the future. Skills like reading, writing, speaking, and math, are crucial in our society, but not as important as being intelligent, curious, caring, and inventive. As one teacher stated, "Maybe one day reading won't be that important. Look, you

can get books on tape, and computers can now read text they present on the screen. Maybe one day reading will supplement other ways of obtaining information." (summary of field notes)

Instead of directly attacking this market rationale as we might in a doctoral seminar, we have found it can be used, at times, to stimulate conversations about what is truly substantive in the education of children who will be living in an, as yet unknown, set of social circumstances.

Another response to the market-driven rationale for schooling has been to focus on its limitations. As Dewey (1976 [1938], p. 49) pointed out long ago,

> The ideal of using the present simply to get ready for the future contradicts itself. It omits, and even shuts out, the very conditions by which a person can be prepared for his future. We always live at the time we live and not at some other time, and only by extracting at each present time the full meaning of each present experience are we prepared for doing the same thing in the future. This is the only preparation which in the long run amounts to anything.

There is much more to life than just working, and directly addressing this issue has been a priority in the schools in which we worked.

> In this session, we asked the faculty if preparation for work was the only responsibility of schools. Immediately, several teachers responded in the negative. They all realized that as important as work is, for many people, it is not the center of their lives. Learning to create a life of meaning, being emotionally happy, self-understanding and expression, having friends, becoming part of a community, and developing family relationships were just a few of the many responses we received from faculty at this school when asked what education should ideally do besides prepare students for future market-driven occupations. In our discussion of how schools should help prepare students for these goals, it soon became clear that the answer was to be found in the existential moment. One teacher said, "If we want students to do this in the future, we need to help them reach these goals today." This comment led the faculty to a discussion of "habits." Specifically, we explored what habits this school should try to instill within their children. Four categories emerged from this conversation: 1) the habits of mind (e.g., being thoughtful, being open to ideas, creating meaning out of our experiences); 2) the habits of voice (e.g., being articulate in written, visual, and oral forms, listening to and understanding others, speaking up); 3) the habits of heart (e.g., caring for oneself and others, recognizing and resisting oppression, developing family, friends, and community); and 4) the habits of work (e.g, persistence, creativity, cooperation, organization, planning). Next, we began the first of several discussions on the pedagogy and curriculum needed to foster these habits. (summary of field notes)

Our final response to this market rationale for schooling was to provide an alternative context for our reform work with these school communities.

Unlike many school reformers who promise better test scores, improved atten-
dance, or more effective discipline, we situated our work within a democratic
ethos. That is, we overtly shared our desire to educate children for the purpose
of preserving, improving, expanding, and deepening our democracy. Whenever the opportunity arose, and was appropriate, we brought this orientation
into our discussions.

> At this point in the discussion, we shared our belief that the most important
> responsibility of schooling is to prepare students to live in our imperfect
> democracy. We suggested that if our goal is to educate children for the
> responsibilities of democratic living, then we wouldn't need to worry about
> preparing them for jobs. That is, the intellectual talents the next generation
> needs to build upon and amplify our democracy incorporate and go beyond
> what is needed to prepare them for the world of work. Democracy is like a
> baton that one generation passes off to the next, and ideally schooling pre-
> pares children for the pick up and for the difficult run ahead of them. It was
> clear that many of the teachers responded enthusiastically to this orientation,
> while a few others felt it was too abstract. (summary of field notes)

Responding to this marketplace rationale for schooling has not been easy. We
have discovered that merely critiquing it as the source of all evil in schools and
society falls largely on deft ears. As previously portrayed, we have chosen to
engage this topic with school communities using several different lines of reasoning. However, our efforts, no matter how successful in a few schools, will
not reverse the power behind this marketplace rationale for schooling. Along
with these school-based projects, it is crucial that this alternative be offered in
the political and cultural realms of our society. Only when there is a broad,
public discourse on this topic will alternatives to this limited rationale for
schooling materialize in ways that will effect our nation's educational system.

High-Stakes Testing

Conservatives have been especially successful in utilizing high-stakes testing
as the dominate form of social control over education in the United States. In
many schools, these tests directly determine curricula, but they also go well
beyond determining (and greatly limiting) what gets taught in our nation's
schools. In addition, as several scholars have noted (Kohn, 2000; McNeil,
2000; Vinson, Gibson and Ross, 2001), high-stakes testing has a tremendous
influence on the nature of instruction, conception of what is considered learning and intelligence, how time is allocated during the school day, student-
teacher relationships, categorizing of children (e.g., tracking, special education), drop-out rates, and our conception of what it means to teach. Worst of
all, as Berlinger and Biddle (1995) convincingly argue, the entire premise
upon which the high-stakes testing movement is based (that is, the failure of
our schools to adequately educate our nation's children as measured quantita-

tively) is little more than a myth, a fabrication by a powerful, conservative coalition of members from the intellectual, intelligentsia, Anglo-American, and bourgeois classes in our society.

Of course, it is not our purpose to explore, as others have done, the negative consequences of high-stakes testing, but rather to illustrate the ways in which these school communities have responded to this conservative project. Unfortunately, from our perspective, too many schools in the United States have responded to high-stakes testing by adopting instructional programs (IPs) that are specifically designed to increase children's scores on them. These programs treat teachers as mere instructional managers. IPs come complete with the curriculum (content), specific learning objectives for each lesson, workbooks, step-by-step instructional procedures to follow, lesson or unit quizzes and exams, template or computer-assisted grading, and remedial worksheets and tests for students who do not pass these exams. From this perspective, teachers are encouraged to become "shop floor" managers, who see to it that their workers (students) use the tools they have been given (IPs) in order to produce a "product" (test scores) in the most efficient manner possible (i.e., cost effective).

There are a few cases of individual teachers who have taken a courageous stand and refused to administer these tests, groups of parents and others who are beginning to organize against these tests (e.g., Parents United for Fair Testing), and educational organizations such as the Rethinking Schools Coalition, the National School Reform Faculty (NSRF), and even the mainstream American Educational Research Association that have spoken out against the use of standardized tests to reward and punish students (and thus sort and categorize the future adults of our society) and schools. However, most of the school communities in which we have worked have been reluctant to confront and challenge these government-initiated assessment projects so directly. Among some teachers, this reluctance is due to a history of poor pedagogy that haunts particular schools:

> Before the state testing started, this school was a mess. We had teachers who said these kids can't learn; who would pass out worksheets and then read their newspaper. No one cared. I mean it, no one—not the principal, not the central administrators, not the parents, not the kids, not the Department of Education, no one. A lot of teachers would say, "If they don't care, why should I?" For years, this school was a pit. If you had a problem, there was no one to help. If you tried to do something worthwhile, everyone else would look at you like you were nuts. "What's the point?" they'd say. No one gave a damn, so why should you work your butt off for nothing? Once the test showed how bad it was, things started to happen. Dr. Orlando [the superintendent], Ms. Black [the principal], and you guys came, and for the first time things started to improve around this place. (Follow-up interview)

However, in most other school communities this reluctance wasn't because they believed testing had significantly improved their schools. For these school communities, it was simply that the time, energy, money, and political activism required to politically and publically challenge high-stakes testing was simply not a social price they were willing to pay. Although we encouraged individuals to become involved with these organizations, within the context of school-based reform projects, we had to explore different types of responses to this politically driven emphasis on quantitative assessment and "accountability." These responses have included discussions and pedagogical practices around topics such as conceptions of what it means to be a teacher, notions of learning and intelligence, who should make curricular and instructional decisions, as well as direct strategies for minimizing the test's influence on the education of children.

Although IPs are popular, we encouraged schools to reject this response to high-stakes testing, and instead suggested that their children would be better educated (as well as perform better on these tests) if they (individually and collectively) develop their own substantive, inquiry-oriented, classroom-based, and school-coordinated curriculum and pedagogy. To our surprise, this vision of teachers and their students studying meaningful topics through authentic learning experiences appealed to many of the schools in which we worked. Much of our time was spent helping these schools visualize, experiment, and reflect on these efforts.

Rather than view themselves as educational technicians who merely manage the curriculum, daily schedule, and children, perhaps the most important response teachers have had to high-stakes testing is re-establishing themselves as creators of curriculum (Goodman, 1986), and therefore assuming responsibility for what gets taught in their classrooms and how it should be taught. While taking into consideration the interests of politicians, parents, colleagues, and especially the children, we supported teachers in their efforts to make all final decisions regarding the curriculum and instruction in their classrooms. Towards this goal, many teachers (in some schools every teacher) developed original, classroom-based, integrated units of study (e.g., language arts, social studies, science, art) in which they selected the topic, generated its themes, selected diverse resources (e.g., books, articles, films, guest speakers, audio recordings, photos and drawings, artifacts) and instructional activities (e.g., reading, writing, performing and visual art projects, simulations, individual and group inquiry projects, cooking) through which students study and express what they have learned about this topic, organized these resources and activities into a unit of study (e.g., contains an introduction, period of study, and conclusion), and assessed students' efforts and quality of work. After creating one or more of these classroom-based units of study, teachers began to understand that they were in a much better position to make curricular and instructional decisions than the writers of IPs.

Equally important to becoming creators of curriculum have been teachers' efforts to directly challenge "deficit thinking" that high-stakes testing encourages (Valencia, 1997). As several authors in Valencia's book point out, deficit thinking has a long and sordid history within education. At its core, deficit thinking assumes children are ignorant and come to school with little knowledge, talent, or skill. The goal of schooling is to determine as specifically as possible what the ideal child should know at any given age, identify exactly what students don't know based upon the previously mentioned template, focus instruction to remediate these weaknesses, test to see if these shortcomings have been corrected, and if not, reinstruct them until they demonstrate competency. Once competency has been achieved students can move onto fixing their next weakness. Deficit thinking has been particularly strong in high-poverty schools, where many educators have assumed that "these kids aren't smart," or "can't learn" (Knapp and Adelman, 1995; Valencia,1997). In response, we had many conversations with school communities similar to the one below:

> At this point in the conversation, we asked why schools emphasize what children don't know and can't do, rather than the opposite. Many suggestions were made including tradition (the way it's always been done), that's the way textbooks are written, our cultural logic (it makes sense), and the emphasis on standardized testing. We then asked the faculty to imagine what schooling might look like if the focus was on identifying what students know, what intellectual and artistic talents they have, ways in which they learn, as well as the contingent needs of our culture to have educated citizens. We then asked, "What might schooling look like if we provided opportunities throughout the academic year for each child to manifest what s/he knows and his/her ways of being intelligent in their classroom?" These questions prompted a long and interesting conversation. In the end, there seemed to be consensus among this group of teachers that it was time to focus their attention not on "if," but "how" their students are smart and knowledgeable. One teacher concluded by saying, "If this project helps us to teach in ways that build on what our kids know and can do, rather than always pointing out what they can't do or don't know, then I'll know this school has really changed." (summary of field notes)

Many of our sessions in these schools focused on resisting influences (including high-stakes testing) that foster deficit thinking among teachers and administrators, and generating ways to educate children that honors many different ways in which children are intelligent (e.g., Armstrong, 2000; Gardner, 1999; Teele, 2000).

Although these conversations helped school communities resist some of the more onerous effects that have emerged from high-stakes testing, they have been most successful in those schools where the politics of high-stakes testing have been directly addressed. In particular, it was necessary to explore ways to "work the system." Many of these schools responded to their high-stakes test by creating a test-taking unit of study. One of the most thoughtful units was developed at Fairchild Elementary School (all proper names are fictitious).

After several sessions, the Curriculum Study Group (CSG) proposed that each teacher develop, using the study guides published by the state's Department of Education, a unit on taking the test. This 4–6 week unit would directly teach the language arts and math content found in the test. In particular, the unit will identify as specifically as possible the exact information that students need to internalize. It will also include many practice tests, using the same type of answer sheet and timed testing used in the state exam. The idea was to help children become familiar with this type of testing and short-term mastery of information. However, the most impressive recommendation from the CSG was the emphasis they placed on putting the state test in a particular context for the students. First, they discussed the need to impress upon the students that this test was not an indication of their intelligence. There are many ways in which one is smart, and this test only touches a few of these. Furthermore, these forms of intelligence covered by the test are not necessarily the most valuable for living a full and happy life. Second, they suggested that the test preparation should be presented like a sporting event. That is, there should be an effort to develop some enthusiasm for the school as a whole to do well on it by having everyone try their best and help each other. However, like a sporting event, the emphasis should be placed on doing the best one can and not whether one "wins" or "loses" (i.e., the final results). Third, it was emphasized that while it was important to do well on the test to avoid summer school, for those who do not pass it, options will be provided so that no one will be retained at the end of the school year simply as a result of their score on this one test. Fourth, and perhaps most important, the principal emphasized that s/he personally did not believe the test measured the quality of education that was occurring in the building, and that this unit of study should be seen as taking the place of the conventional "drilling for skills" that many students face all year long. The central purpose of the unit is to free up the rest of the year to practice the type of pedagogy that s/he and the teachers have decided is best for their students. If the school doesn't do well on the test, the principal volunteered to take "the heat." (summary of field notes)

The trepidation that this test caused was very real in the minds of most school communities. In an effort to ameliorate their fears, it was often necessary to contact schools that have improved their scores using an inquiry-orientated, rather than a "drill-for-skills" pedagogy to show others that it can be done. As portrayed in chapter 3, in one school the CSG and principal visited the state testing officials.

Another response to high-stakes testing in many of these schools was for someone within the school community to become deeply knowledgeable about the ways in which quantitative information can be manipulated to support their academic program:

Today the Leadership Team discussed the findings from the state competency test. At first glance it seemed as if the school had not improved as much as they had expected (although the scores had definitely gone up) given that this was the third year of our reform project. However, then the counselor shared the findings she got when she began to factor out several variables. For example, when she factored in only those students who had stayed in the building for the last three years (and thus had the full benefit of the reforms) the results were astounding. These students' scores had improved an average of nearly 20 percent over the last time they took the test. Students who had been in the school for the last two years also averaged higher scores than students who had been in the building for less than two years. Similarly, when only the scores of students who had been absent less than 5 out of the last 180 days of school were tabulated, they also had scores well above the state's average. (summary of field notes)

Learning how to utilize the data received from these tests was extremely important for those schools that were resisting the tendency to adopt IPs and thus have their curriculum completely aligned with these questionable tests.

Finally, only one school in which we worked attempted to develop an alternative form of assessment as a response to the state's high-stakes testing program.

Several years ago, Broadview Elementary was given permission to start a magnet school based upon Howard Gardner's theory of multiple intelligences. Instead of having traditional courses (e.g., English, social studies, science, reading, math), they had class periods that corresponded to his forms of intelligence. All classes were coordinated by a school-wide 9-week theme. Unfortunately, after two years the children's test scores did not improve significantly from when the school was based on the traditional curriculum and instructional patterns. However, the faculty felt certain that the education they were providing was far superior to what the school traditionally offered. They decided to develop an alternative to the state's testing program of assessment. The centerpiece of their program will be a video portfolio of each child. The plan is to video each child and their work throughout the school year and keep this visual record of each child's academic progress. The faculty then discussed how they can use these videos to resist pressure from the board to look only at the state's test to evaluate the quality of the students' learning and thus the quality of the school's education. (summary of field notes)

Subsequently, this school was able to resist calls for its closure despite its failure to raise the children's scores on the state's test, in part, due to these video portfolios. However, these types of responses to high-stakes testing have been few and far between.

Under the NCLB Act, the pressure on schools to align their curricula to the state's test, and to adopt a drill/memorize/quiz ritual of instruction has never been greater. Although it was possible for individual schools to "talk back" to the high-stakes testing movement, clearly a more broad-based public movement is necessary. As scholars, we rarely have this type of access to the public, and educators in the schools and teachers' unions find it difficult to publically condemn this movement due to the perception of being "self-serving." What is needed is the creation of a broad-based coalition with a single focus on publicizing the negative consequences of this political effort to socially control the education of our young people. What makes this task particularly difficult is the fact that the vast majority of developing and modern societies (including the few socialist countries left in the world) have all adopted a program of education that includes both a national curriculum and a system of standardized testing for the purposes of sorting children based upon their scores. This agenda item is one that, unfortunately, looks like we will have to struggle with for many more years.

Re-establishing Normative Culture

Although it often does not seem so, the last half century has not been particularly kind to those in our society who wish to retain the hegemony of bourgeois, Anglo-European, patriarchal cultural norms. First, the GI bill made it possible for members of the working class to attend college and thus enter the intellectual and intellegentsia classes; then the Civil Rights, Black Power, and Ethnic Awareness Movements broke down long-standing barriers for people of color; now the vision of a pluralistic rather than assimilationist culture has further disrupted our notions of what it means to be an American; and of course, the Women's and Gay Rights Movements have caused us to fundamentally rethink the gender identities within our nation.

It is little wonder then, that conservatives have struggled to re-establish the pre–World War II norms of our society, and schools have been one of the primary battlegrounds where this contest has occurred. Educators such as William Bennett (1992), Chester Finn and Diane Ravitch (1984), E. D. Hirsch (1988) and members of various classes such as the Fundamentalist Christians (Bates, 1993; Kaplan, 1994) and individuals such as those involved in the "English only" movement (Crawford, 1992, 2000) have fought hard to reclaim the previously mentioned cultural norms through the schooling of our children. This push has only been partially successful, but has been clearly felt within each of the schools in which we have worked.

Since many of these schools served primarily children of color or those with Spanish-speaking heritages, we encouraged faculty to embrace the role schooling can play in our move towards pluralism.

> Today the Curriculum Study Group discussed how it can help teachers infuse the ethnic heritages of the students (which are predominately African American and Hispanic American) and more gender balance into their language arts and social studies curriculum. Several suggestions were made about how to locate children's literature and other resources that reflect the struggles and contributions of these historically marginalized people in our society. People agreed to explore several potential distributors of these mate-

rials, such as Cobblestone Publishing, National Council for the Social Studies, Rethinking Schools, Teaching History and Ourselves, and the Interracial Council of Books for Children. One teacher asked if the CSG was planning to suggest the elimination of conventional history and literature, and expressed concern if this was the case. This initiated a discussion on how to approach the teaching of pluralism in ways that value our ethnic and gender diversity, but in a way that did not destroy our identity as a nation. The discussion ended without a clear resolution, but one suggestion did receive particular attention. One teacher suggested that we see ourselves as a people who come from different ancestral heritages, and who have struggled *together* to create a society that honors our differences. "We are bonded and share a common identity by this ongoing struggle with each other." The meeting ended with one individual volunteering to explore staff development options on this topic. (summary of field notes)

Although conservatives have voiced concerns over the emerging pluralism of our culture, this is one arena where educators and the population in general are, for the most part, firmly committed to moving beyond the myth of our society as a "melting pot," and recognizing that schools have an important role to play in facilitating this shift in our collective perspective.

Perhaps the most difficult issue related to the conservative push for re-establishing the Anglo-European, male hegemony has concerned the teaching of English. The vast majority of the students in these schools did not speak the dialect of English that is currently spoken by those in power. Most of these children speak an urban Ebonic dialect or a Spanish dialect of English at home. While there was near universal agreement on the importance of teaching what many call "standard English," there were significant differences over how teaching this subject area should be contextualized:

At today's meeting we discussed several articles concerning the teaching of English by Lisa Delpit, Gloria Ladson-Billings, John Ogbu, and others. The reactions to these articles were diverse. Some of the most contentious ideas were that there was no "correct" way to speak or write English (or any language). That is, the notion of "standard English" was, in fact, a myth. Instead, there are simply different dialects of a given language. In any particular culture during any specific time in history, it is possible to identify what might be called a "dialect of power," that is, a particular way of speaking and writing by people who are currently in positions of social, economic, or political power. These authors suggest that it is extremely important to situate the teaching of English within this particular context so that children whose families do not speak the "dialect of power" at home will understand that they are not learning "the correct" way to speak at school, but are being asked to become *bi-dialectic*. Once students learn this "dialect of power," they will have access, as adults, to powerful institutions in society, and will then be in a better position to alter this society for the purposes of personal fulfillment and social justice. Several teachers felt these articles really "spoke to them," and understood the important point they were making. Others felt the articles were "off base," that there was a "correct" way to speak and write English, that English is a language while Ebonics was a dialect, and that children need to learn the "right way" to speak and write. At the end of the discussion, we set up a time to meet with those teachers who wanted to explore strategies for teaching "standard English" as a dialect. (summary of field notes)

Although the teaching of reading, speaking, and writing English is considered paramount in perhaps every elementary school in our country, it is particularly problematic in schools where the children do not speak or hear the dialect of power in their homes and neighborhoods. The creative challenge for these teachers is to explore how to teach children a command of the "dialect of power," while at the same time validating the children's "home dialect."

To summarize, there are many issues that progressive-thinking educational reformers need to address in response to the onslaught of policies imposed upon schools by conservative politicians, lay people, and educators. The issues portrayed in this paper (e.g., privatization of education, the market rationale for schooling, high-stakes testing, and the re-establishment of Anglo-European cultural norms) are just a few of the many topics that need to be carefully explored by school communities if they are to resist this conservative agenda and create meaningful educational experiences for themselves and our children.

REFLECTIONS ON CHAPTER 5: UNDERSTANDING POWER AS A KEY TO SCHOOL-BASED REFORM

Some scholars who explore the relationship between neoliberalism and education either unwittingly or unintentionally present a rather dooms-day vision of the future (e.g., McLaren and Farahmandpur, 2000). The impression is that unless there is some sort of major revolutionary change in power among nation states and in global economic and political systems, the opportunities for progressive education are minimal. On a grand scale this assessment might be correct. However, aside from breeding a sense of powerlessness among school communities, we question the usefulness and efficacy of such scholarship. However, these social, economic, and political forces do have a direct and significant impact upon the schooling of our children, and it would be a serious mistake to ignore the dangerous influences that school communities must face today. As discussed in this chapter, the challenge before us is to work with these communities to resist the conservative influences now descending upon our schools and children. It is useful to terminate this chapter by discussing an issue that we have found crucial if resistance is to be effective.

As portrayed in chapter 3, we directly raised questions of power with the members of the school communities. The implications of understanding power related to schooling and the current conservative ethos dominating our country is significant. As previously mentioned, much of this agenda emerged from sectors of our society other than education. In particular, the educational policies of this agenda have emerged primarily from the political, religious, and economic spheres of our society. Most progressive members of school communities, scholars, and school reformers have little contact with those who work within these realms of society. This lack of connection is most unfortunate, and needs to be seriously addressed. It is crucial that coalitions be built between progressive educators and those individuals who currently work in the economic (e.g., corporate managers, union officials) and political (e.g., politicians, lobbyists) and other (e.g., media) spheres of our society. For example, on May 5, 2001 there was a nation-wide protest against high-stakes testing. Similarly, before his untimely death, Senator Wellstone introduced a bill that would have required school districts to regularly conduct studies to determine the impact high-stakes testing has on the quality of teachers' and students' educational experiences or risk losing federal funding. Although working among school communities is imperative in the face of this latest push by conservatives, we need to reach out to those who work in other spheres of our society, and form a broad-based coalition dedicated to altering the most pernicious aspects of the conservative agenda.

CHAPTER 6

Conclusion:
Reflections from the Field

This book has portrayed Harmony Education Center's reform work in numerous schools and explored a number of issues that emerged from these efforts. As stated in the first chapter, we place our work within the reform leftist tradition found within the progressive history of the United States. In particular, we view this work as contributing to the efforts of other educators and cultural workers who have attempted to make (and continue to work towards making) our society more deeply democratic, socially just, equitable, and prosperous. Although HEC focuses its efforts almost exclusively on the educational realm of society (see chapter 1), we are acutely aware that what happens in one sphere of society is influenced by and, in turn, influences the other significant realms that exist in a given polity at a particular point in time. As mentioned in chapter 2, our aim has not been to present this work as a model for others to mimic. Rather, we hope that it provides images and ideas that others might find informative, thought-provoking, and useful in their own endeavors.

Throughout much of the last thirty years, and in particular since the Bush administration came into power, it has not been easy to work as a progressive educator or educational change agent. The United States has a relatively long and deep conservative tradition and electorate, and working to alter this conservative orientation towards schooling has never been easy. Fortunately, there continues to be determined individuals and groups who refuse to turn a blind eye to the negative consequences that have fallen upon our schools (especially those located in high-poverty communities) during this latest conservative resurgence in our country. This book represents a small contribution to the ongoing progressive social, political, and educational discourse that refuses to recede in spite of the difficult times in which we find ourselves. Although each chapter "speaks" for itself, there are a few additional subjects that warrant further attention and are thus the focus of this concluding chapter.

THE NATURE OF SCHOOL-BASED REFORM

In the United States, there is a tradition of valuing local reform projects in schools, government, or any number of other social institutions. As stated in chapter 2, school-based reform suggests that teachers and principals conceptualize, initiate, and develop the alterations that take place in a given school. However, not all school-based reform efforts are the same. Most actually share many of the same aims and values as "top-down" reformers (e.g., Maeroff, 1988; Mann, 1983). Teachers and principals are "given" more autonomy and power, but typically within very narrow limits and purposes, such as being allowed to determine technical questions of *how* a given curriculum is taught in order to increase test scores on standardized tests. We share the view with other democratic-thinking reformers that schools need to be altered for more substantive purposes than meeting the interests of those groups who currently dominate our political, economic, social, and educational institutions.

As previously mentioned (see chapter 2), school reform is best viewed as a form of *discursive practice*. Michel Foucault suggests that discourse has great power in bringing about a particular social reality. He argues that systems of discourse reflect and at times become alternative systems of power. Discourse is used by individuals to distinguish "truth" from "falsehood," thus significantly influencing the way in which individuals think, feel, and act in given social settings. During a given period of history, a society (or specific institutions in a society such as schools) will have a dominant discourse or "regime of truth" (Dreyfus and Rabinow, 1983; Rajchman, 1985). For example, as previously mentioned, many school-reform efforts have been contextualized within a "marketplace" rationality. Schools need to be reformed to meet the corporate needs of society and thus "beat" our global competitors. This discourse has successfully silenced other rationalities for reforming schools such as those that enhance the democracy in which we live.

Bloom (1992) provides insight into how these dominant discourses function. Drawing upon Mikhail Bakhtin's work, she makes a distinction between authoritative and internally persuasive discourses. Authoritative discourse demands our acknowledgment of it. It is presented in formal, hierarchical contexts and in such a way as to make it almost taboo to question it. As Bakhtin states, its power is such that we bind ourselves to it merely because it is spoken with such authority, "independent of any power it might have to persuade us internally. . . . It is, so to speak, the words of the fathers" (Bloom, 1992: 314). Internally persuasive discourse "engages us from within, rather than imposes itself from without" (Bloom, 1992: 315). Internally persuasive discourses enable us to reflect upon ideas in ways that make them our own. Separating from authoritative discourse is rarely easy or complete. "The process of gaining subjective voice is situated problematically . . . within the dialogical tensions between authoritative and internally persuasive discourses" (Bloom, 1992: p. 315).

School-based reforms rooted within a democratic ethos can be viewed as a process that enables teachers and principals to discover and nurture their internally persuasive discourse through critical collaboration. Typically, these discourses not only involve explorations into the daily problems and difficulties found in a given school, but also the social and pedagogical values, assumptions, and presuppositions of the teachers, the principal, the district administration, and the local community. Rather than merely responding to the popular slogans of and calls for improvements, school-based reform encourages teachers and principals to set their own agenda (e.g., Klein, 1989). Viewing educational reform as a discursive practice provides opportunities for teachers and principals to directly challenge current regimes of truth, develop their own internally persuasive understandings of education, and then act upon these understandings. This notion of school reform can be seen as a form of educational praxis; that is, a process by which teachers', parents', administrators' and students' conceptual analysis of pedagogy and society is used to inform their practice, followed by reflection upon their practice in an effort to inform their on-going conceptualizing. To engage in educational reform as discursive practice is to perpetually construct a working analysis of schooling and social life as the foundation for what occurs in given schools. However, as educational change agents, we have been confronted by several issues that have become the focus of our reflection.

EMERGENT ISSUES

As previously mentioned, the focus of this chapter is to reflect upon a number of issues that have emerged from our work with teachers, administrators, support staff, and parents involved in school-based reform. We began our work with fairly naive notions about the work of school reform. As these issues surfaced, we became (sometimes painfully) aware of the complexity or "messiness" of the task we were undertaking. Unfortunately, we have more questions than absolute answers related to these issues. Rather than search for closure, our intention has been to initiate dialogue and further understanding of the work that we, as external change agents, can engage in during school-based reform efforts.

The Role of External Change Agents

Since teachers and principals are at the core of school-based reform, one might ask what role can external change agents have in such projects. Does "school-based" mean that teachers and principals must "go it alone?" Certainly, there are powerful examples of teachers, such as the publishers of *Rethinking Schools*, who have initiated and sustained several significant reforms in the Milwaukee Schools without outside assistance (Peterson, 1993). Our position is that while external change agents may not be necessary, their involvement in itself does not violate the spirit of school-based reform. If this position is valid, then the question of what role they play becomes critical. In our initial search to learn about the role of external change agents in school reform, we found that much of this work has been designed "consciously or unconsciously in assumptions rooted in bureaucratic control" of teachers (Sachs and Logan, 1990).

The most prevalent role that external change agents assume is that of a "merchant." This "purchase" approach to school reform involves identifying particular information that teachers need and then hiring an expert to provide the necessary "merchandise." Perhaps the most popular example of this merchant-consumer relationship during the last two decades in the United States has been similar to Madeline Hunter's curriculum-planning model. In these types of situations, teachers are told that the way to improve education is to follow the steps developed in various instructional models. Teachers then take a series of workshops that teach teachers the mechanics of these models. Once teachers learn what to do, they are expected to follow "the program." It is common for schools to view external change agents in this light. For example, we often have been approached by given schools because they have heard about our expertise in curriculum development or classroom management. As mentioned earlier, our initial meetings are often devoted to clarifying our values and relationship with these schools. In fact, this purchase approach to reform is so commonplace that it is difficult for many to think of different types of relationships between external change agents and school personnel.

> Today we received an invitation to participate in Penny Lane Elementary School's first ever, two-day fall retreat. Last year we helped develop a democratic vision for their school and participated in a classroom-based curriculum development project. Although we were pleased that they decided to take our suggestion (given at the end-of-the-year meeting last spring) to have this fall retreat, we were still troubled by its format. At the spring meeting, we were very direct about what we thought they needed to do in order to make their vision a reality. Throughout last year, Penny Lane's teachers and principal spent almost all of their professional development funds and time taking numerous workshops covering a broad range of topics. We suggested that they stop or greatly reduce the time spent in these workshops, and instead spend their professional development time with each other, sharing ideas for the future, working through problems they identify along the way, and building the type of program they had envisioned earlier in the school year. Although they agreed with us and seemed excited by this new orientation to professional development, this fall retreat is merely another series of workshops. We have been asked to conduct a session on "teacher-student relationships." (summary of field notes)

There are literally hundreds of school-reform "merchants" that sell their "reforms" for everything from disciplining students, to curriculum planning, to teaching particular subjects (e.g., math, spelling, sex, drugs), to cooperative learning, to test-taking. The acceptance of this purchase approach is so complete that even when teachers and principals, such as those at Penny Lane

Elementary School, agree that an alternative approach is needed, it still dominates the way in which we think about school consultants.

Another common role that external agents assume is that of a medical examiner. The medical model of school reform is often seen as valuable in cases when the performance of a particular school has declined (as measured on standardized tests scores) and consultants are brought into the school to determine the nature of the problems and correct them. Departments of education associated with state governments often utilize the medical model to evaluate schools. In these cases, consultants come into a school and examine it much like a doctor examines a patient. The goal of the medical examiner is to diagnose the school's "illness" and then recommend the appropriate "treatment." For example, the state of Florida resorts to this tactic in schools that fail to raise their children's test scores (e.g., Yendol-Silva, 2003).

In spite of their popularity, we found these roles to be problematic. First, they are based upon an assumption that the difficulties of a given school are usually isolated from other aspects of schooling and spheres of society (see chapter 1). As a result, the solution is also fairly easily determined and implemented by having teachers and principals follow the directives of the designated expert. Thus, school reforms can be initiated with relatively little commitment on the part of the external reformer who typically interacts with the faculty for a short period of time. S/he comes, presents his/her information or analysis, and s/he goes. In each case, the educational reform is viewed as a process of "fixing" schools. There is little recognition given to the view that educational reform can be based upon the visionary thinking or reflection upon previous experiences of teachers and principals. Second, the merchant and medical examiner roles assume that teachers and principals play a relatively passive function in determining the scope and substance of either a given school's problems, or more importantly, its possibilities. As several scholars (e.g., Yendol-Silva, 2003; Wood, 2003) have noted, these approaches to school improvement often have an opposite effect due to the demoralization that occurs among many of the faculty members.

In contrast, when working as external change agents, we try to maintain as much as possible our role as *participants* who engage teachers and principals in the previously mentioned discursive practice. However, in the school-based reform projects discussed in this book, the previous participatory role is slightly altered into *informed participants*. After all, we are asked to work with given schools because the teachers and principal view us as informed in particular ways that will help them. As we state to the schools with which we work, our participation is informed by thirty years of democratic schooling experience found at Harmony School, as well as our understanding of progressive discourse among educational scholars (see chapter 2). This role of informed participant is perhaps most clearly manifested at school retreats:

At the retreat today we broke into small groups to generate a list of the school's problems and possibilities. When we came together for our general discussion, it became clear that this faculty felt overwhelmed by their students. Many of these children came from the low-income section of town, and although they weren't officially labeled as such, the teachers referred to them in general as "at risk students." Too many students, they said, came to school angry, often in significant emotional pain, and skeptical of teachers' intensions. These conditions made it extremely difficult, they said, to teach. After exploring their perceptions in some depth, we asked them to describe the type of changes they would like to see in this school, and challenged them to view these children as assets rather than as liabilities in making this school become a reality. The discussion took on a different tone after this question. The picture the teachers drew was of a school in which children and teachers felt safe, emotionally and physically. It was a school in which children learn to work through their pain and anger rather than express them in antisocial interactions. We asked them to consider that everything they "knew" about "at risk" children were myths (e.g., they can't learn; assume responsibility; respect themselves, other children, and adults; solve problems). This concept of "myths" became a focus for the rest of our discussion. Today, we began a conversation with this faculty about how to create a school that would challenge the social, political, and educational "myths" that surround the education of "at risk" students. (summary of field notes)

As informed participants, we make a special effort to facilitate conversations about teachers' ideals, dreams, and visions of education, and the relationship between these concepts and their images of a "good" society (Onore and Lester, 1993). Rather than coming to a school as experts with the "problem" (e.g., teachers don't plan correctly) and the "solution" (Hunter's model) already determined, we seek to participate with teachers and others in a series of conversations into the nature of a given faculty's values and the context within which they operate.

From this perspective, it is vital for school personnel to identify the problems and possibilities of their own schools, rather than relying on external diagnosticians. Even when we recognize a problem and have ideas about how it could be solved soon after entering a given school, we are careful to avoid sharing our speculations prematurely. First, we have come to realize that we might be incorrect in our assessment. For example, in our early meetings with Hathaway Elementary School, the teachers and principal informed us that as part of their reform program they decided to have all students and staff wear "uniforms" (white t-shirts with the school logo and navy blue pants, shorts, or skirts). At first we viewed this decision as unwise, since it seemed to reflect an ethos of social conformism that would strip students of their individuality. However, as a "magnet" school, students came to this building from all over a large metropolitan area. The student body included children from vastly different social, racial, and economic backgrounds. The decision to have uniforms came from a sensitivity on the part of both teachers and parents to those students who live in poverty and who would be spending hours each day next to children who live in affluence. Uniforms in this situation were viewed as a way to help children go beyond the "clothes that people wear" and discover other attributes upon which to establish friendships. In short, uniforms at this school promoted the development of authentic relationships among the students and a sense of community within the school. At the same time, teachers were sensitive to our concerns and were quick to affirm students' individuality as reflected in their work and personalities. As we look back on our initial assessment, we can see how easy it is to let one's ideology degenerate into dogma.

Second, even if we are correct, premature disclosing of our analysis has, at times, resulted in defensiveness or unnecessary dependency on us as the people with the "answer." As informed participants, we see our role as drawing attention to practical or theoretical aspects of a particular problem or providing alternative visions of schooling that teachers may not have considered, but our primary goal is to help teachers and other school personnel gain insight into what is going on around them, within them, and between them and others in their school.

Although our vision of informed participants has shaped the way in which we prefer to view ourselves, in actual situations we have learned that the distinctions between our role and the role of external change agents embedded within the "purchase" and "medical" models of school reform have become blurred. For example, after several conversations at Dyer Elementary School, the teachers decided to create, rather than merely manage, the curriculum in their classrooms. However, they expressed reservations concerning their abilities to fulfill this responsibility. Just having conversations about the nature of curriculum clearly was not enough for these teachers. Responding to this concern required us to adopt a role similar to that of merchants. We conducted several sessions to inform these teachers about one way to design (from a critical perspective) school-based curriculum (Goodman, 1986), and we provided assistance as they developed new types of classes and taught thematic units of study throughout the school year.

At times, we have assumed roles that we initially never considered, such as serving as intermediaries to state officials.

> Today we focused on the ISTEP [Indiana State Test of Educational Performance] exam and the constraining impact it is having on teachers' thinking about curricular reform. These teachers are considering completely replacing the traditional social studies and science curriculum with integrated, thematic, classroom-based units of study, and to replace the "developmental skills" language arts curriculum with a "whole language" approach. However, if several students fail the ISTEP (which is based upon the traditional curriculum) then they feel that the central administration might withdraw support from and

cancel their "experimental program." As one teacher said, "What if I stop teaching spelling, and the students fail spelling on the ISTEP?" We spent much of our time today exploring their specific fears and the nature of risk-taking inherent in substantive curricular reform. After a lengthy discussion, they decided (with our encouragement) to confront the Department of Education with their concerns. (summary of field notes)

After this meeting, we wrote a memo outlining the teachers' proposed curriculum and major apprehensions related to the reforms. Next, we set up a meeting with the testing officials in the Indiana Department of Education. In this meeting we helped the teachers and principal articulate their curricular visions and the impact that the ISTEP was having on the school's reform efforts (see chapter 4).

In addition to serving as intermediaries, we have assumed the role of referral agents, connecting teachers and principals to individuals with "special knowledge" of a given situation.

> We stayed late today at the request of the principal. As an African American, she is having difficulty with two European American teachers who she suspects are unconsciously prejudiced or insensitive in the way they view poor, African American boys who "act up" in class. From her perspective, these teachers are too quick to judge these young boys as "bad." Her heart goes out especially to these and other Afro-American boys who she feels have suffered greatly especially during the last few years due to poverty and racism, and she is disturbed that these teachers do not seem to be conscious of how their attitudes contribute to these children's oppression. She feels that in all other aspects and with all other types of children, these are excellent teachers and by most people's standards they are not "racist." This makes it harder for her when she sees them treating these boys with (from her perspective) disdain. What is making this particularly difficult is that she is at a point in her life when it is becoming increasingly difficult for her to keep silent, as she has throughout her life when interacting with Euro-Americans, about "racism in our society." She recognizes that her anger makes it more difficult to address this issue within her role as principal, and tonight she asked for help in solving this problem. We asked her to give us some time to think about how we might help. Later, during our debriefing session, we quickly realized that, as Euro-Americans, we could not address this problem adequately alone. After some consideration, we proposed to her (and she agreed) that we get together with four or five individuals from a variety of ethnic and racial backgrounds whom we know have addressed similar issues in their occupations, and with them generate some ideas that may help her. (summary of field notes)

Depending upon specific needs of a school, we have assumed many roles in working with teachers and principals including as inservice educators (e.g., teaching specific instructional strategies such as those related to "whole language" instruction); participants in curriculum brainstorming sessions (generating curricular topics and content); librarians (finding and providing resources for specific instructional projects); grant writers and editors; facilitators for individual and group problem-solving sessions; mediators of conflicts among teachers, principals, central administrators, and/or parents; coordinators for school networking; public advocates for the schools with whom we work; and liaisons to other teachers and administrators involved in similar reform efforts (e.g., the Institute for Democracy in Education, Center for Collaborative Education, Coalition for Essential Schools).

Although we prefer the role of informed participants, our work with schools has drawn us into a variety of roles and responsibilities. Given our critical view of school-reform "merchants," it was uncomfortable for us to admit that in some situations there is a need for external change agents to assume this type of role. Were we a different kind of merchant than Madeline Hunter when we taught these teachers our critical approach to curriculum design, and if so, what made us different? Were our referrals to people with special knowledge legitimizing the need for experts? Does assuming roles other than informed participants violate the grassroots relationship between external change agents, principals and teachers? As will be discussed, this role diversity brought forth several other issues for us to consider.

Ideology and Power

Another issue that emerged from our work concerns the relationship between ideology and power. Conventional approaches to school-based reform assume an ideologically neutral position for external change agents. At first, it would seem necessary for external reformers to present themselves as individuals without an educational agenda of their own; thus positioning themselves as neutral and indicating that it is not their business to tell a school what its purposes, goals, or actions should be. From this perspective, the external reformer is there to assist the teachers and principals in doing what *they* believe is best. If schools want to raise children's test scores on standardized tests, or merely need help in making the scope and sequence of its curriculum more efficient and quantitatively accountable, then external reformers should uncritically accept the value of these goals. From this value-neutral perspective, if a school wants help in determining what its goals are to be, reformers would facilitate (using various communication design processes) the articulation of these goals, but they would not advocate for any particular set of goals or values for this school to adopt.

At times when particular ideas are presented by value-neutral school consultants, their suggestions are situated within a "research says" context. Take, for instance, Mory and Salisbury's statement that grassroots school reform be based upon "*our* [my emphasis] current knowledge about learning, instructional design, child development, and management practices" (1992, p. 7).

During the last several decades, there has been a plethora of reformers who, based upon the latest research on the type of schools our society needs for the twenty-first century, stand ready to help schools prepare for the coming information-technology age (e.g., Banathy, 1992; Reigeluth, 1987). The impression given is that particular reforms are advocated as a result of consensual research findings rather than as a reflection of ideology. However, anyone familiar with educational scholarship understands all too well that within any given field of study one would be hard pressed to find consensus, and research can easily be found to support any number of educational reforms. In reality, external reformers' ideologies are used consciously or unconsciously to screen not only the fields of study (e.g., instructional design vs. curriculum studies), but also the specific research that one brings to school reform. External school reformers are no more protected from political and social biases than other individuals. By coating their suggestions in terms of scientific neutrality, they amplify the importance of their views, and place teachers and principals in the position of passive knowledge consumers. Using "scientific findings" as the basis of a school-reform project is particularly insidious because the biases inherent in such comments are difficult to detect and are unlikely to be challenged by teachers and principals who are often unfamiliar with educational research. Instead, these biases themselves become part of a stifling practice of scientific school reform. Although external change agents armed with research firmly believe that as long as they are not conscious of any ideological agenda they are neutral and objective, in fact, they are only unconscious.

In our conversations with faculty, we have made an effort to be openly ideological, or what Pink and Hyde (1991) refer to as being "proactive." As discussed in chapters 1 and 2, our work in schools is grounded in continuously evolving social and pedagogical values and visions concerning the relationship between school and society, epistemology, curriculum development, power relationships in schools, learning processes, the nature of childhood, and organizational structure. As previously mentioned, we share Dewey's (1966 [1916]) view that education should help people live more democratic lives. As a way of life, democracy implies an appreciation for individual diversity balanced by a sense of social responsibility for the common good. We view our work with teachers and principals as an opportunity to create an education that will empower them and their students to build a more democratic and socially just society than presently exists in the United States (Goodman, 1992).

To be forthcoming about our own pedagogical and social agenda, we articulate in general terms our ideology during initial meetings with teachers and principals. We suggest to teachers and principals that one of the things we have to offer is our perspective. Practically speaking, we have found it useful to discuss our values soon after initial contact has been made so that principals and teachers can make informed decisions about whether they wish to work with us. As a result, we are rarely in the position of spending a great amount of time in a given school only to discover later that the teachers and principal have a significantly different agenda than our own:

> We have now met with the principal and/or teachers on three different occasions, and it seems clear that we will not be working closely together. Their entire school-reform project is based upon an "outcome-based" educational philosophy, a perspective we clearly do not share. They seem to have little interest in exploring educational reform from alternative philosophical "landscapes," as Maxine Greene would say. (summary of field notes)

This openly ideological stance is perhaps a distinctive feature of HEC's approaches to school-based reform.

In reflection, however, we have come to recognize an intrinsic contradiction and paradox in our work. The question before us is, how do we remain true to our convictions to reformulate education towards a social, liberal, and critical democracy, and at the same time follow a course of "bottom-up" educational transformation in which teachers and principals assume the primary responsibility for reforming their schools? To insist that teachers and principals adopt our ideology as a precondition to working together is a contradiction if one also advocates for school-based reform. Although we are committed to a democratic vision of schools and society, we want teachers and principals to create their own goals and visions on behalf of their students and community.

We have struggled to create relationships that allow us not only to facilitate teachers' and principals' voices, but also to share openly our own views and values related to any given topic. We have employed several strategies to establish this open dialogue without having us, as external reformers, be viewed as the experts with the answers. In our initial contacts with a school, we consciously present our ideology as broadly conceived, tentative, and evolving, rather than as a grand theory or regime of truth. We communicate, verbally and through our actions, our belief that all ideas, values, and visions, including our own, are inherently vulnerable. In discussing specific issues with teachers and principals, our contributions are presented as simply our ideas that are not inherently better or worse than the ideas of the people with whom we are working. To further guard against the possibility of our views becoming canon, we encourage teachers and/or principals to make all final decisions about a given situation in subsequent meetings without our direct involvement. By emphasizing the power of teachers and principals to make final decisions, we are free to express our views with minimal risk of being coercive.

However, the dynamics of power found in school reform situations are not so easily understood or resolved. As previously mentioned, once involved with a particular school, the distinctions between various approaches to school reform become obscured. As a result, the nature of power imbedded within these relationships can take unsuspecting turns. Ideally, if we have any influence with teachers and principals, it is because our ideas are internally persuasive to them, rather than because we speak with authority. However, in some circumstances, we have found it valuable to be placed in the role of experts even though we ideologically reject this position and have employed the previously mentioned strategies. For example, after spending considerable time at Dogwood Elementary School, it was not uncommon for the teachers and the principal to present their ideas about particular matters (e.g., curriculum content, instructional activity, relationship with students or parents) for our feedback. In these situations, we often found ourselves legitimizing the teachers' and the principal's views. If we supported their ideas, then their confidence increased. When we offered them critical feedback, they often modified their thinking or actions according to our analysis of the situation. By placing us in the position of experts, we were able in many situations to furnish these teachers with authoritative endorsement or suggestions for what they intuitively believed were good educational practices, curricular content, or social visions, but which had never been sanctioned by anyone in power (district superordinates or individuals with advanced university degrees) prior to our involvement. During the more than twelve years we worked in schools, we often legitimized teachers' aspirations to develop thematically integrated courses of study, to employ alternative methods for assessing students' learning, to emphasize environmental education in their curriculum, and to develop approaches to discipline that promote students' ethic of caring and community. In addition, these individuals have embraced our suggestions to ground their work within an ethos of democracy, to become creators of the curriculum in their school, to establish instructional practices and graduation requirements that cultivate and reflect children's multiple intelligences (Gardner, 1999), to structure classes that allow multi-aged groupings of children, to broaden the school governance to include students, and to teach about people in the world who have been historically marginalized. When inquiries are made about their program, these teachers and principals have at times justified their work by invoking our names, Indiana University, or the Harmony Education Center.

From our perspective, teachers were internally persuaded by our ideas on a variety of issues. They did not, after all, agree with everything we said and often significantly altered our suggestions in ways that made them their own. However, it was in our role as experts that made it possible to legitimize their school's reforms. In this way teachers and principals utilized our involvement to gain more autonomy for themselves and their school (see chapter 3). However, from another perspective, our interaction could be viewed as teachers once again deferring to outside authority. Instead of being internally affirmed or having achieved authoritative support for their ideas, teachers might be seen as simply submitting their ideas for approval, or worse, as merely following directives, which ultimately reifies the "service" role that has kept them largely powerless.

Our uneasiness with this latter perspective is exacerbated by the gender and racial composition of the participants. Nearly all of the teachers and the principals in these schools were women and roughly divided across racial lines (50 percent African-American, and 50 percent Euro-American). Although our work with these schools often included visitations to Harmony School and some consultation meetings that included Harmony teachers and students, in many of these sessions the informed participants were Euro-American men. It would not be difficult to conclude, as some teachers at Harmony School have done, that our relationship with schools implicitly bolsters a system of patriarchy (and possibly racism), which affirms white men's control over women and people of color:

> At today's meeting, a few teachers (at Harmony) voiced their objection to the fact that the "directors" of the Center [and hence the individuals most involved in school-reform projects] were all [white] men. As one teacher stated, "We need to look at the implications of the 'feminist critique' as it relates to the structure of the Center." Questions were raised as to why teachers are not more directly involved in the Center's consultation work. In response, it was pointed out that the "directors" were donating their work, as consultants, to the Center, and until the Center becomes more financially solvent, it didn't seem fair to ask teachers to donate their time to it. The meeting ended with the creation of a Center governing committee that would include at least 50 percent women. (summary of field notes)

What role have we played in these schools? Did we help liberate or oppress these educators? Does situating oneself as an expert always lead to the disenfranchisement or can it facilitate, in certain circumstances, the empowerment of teachers? How do we come to understand the power relationships embedded in such situations? Did the fact that it was the teachers and principals in many of these schools who gave us the power to act as experts (rather than our professional status or position as superordinates in the district hierarchy) make our interactions empowering versus disenfranchizing for these individuals? Is it significant that our role as experts only emerged after working together for an extended period of time and after a meaningful level of trust was established between ourselves and the teachers and principals? Although the teachers and principals have often indicated to us that our interactions have left them feeling empowered, have they been victims of false consciousness, unable to recognize their own oppression? There are many subtle dynamics at work in these situations, and the value of one's work with people is not easily evident.

Questions of Commitment

In addition to our concerns about power, we also have questions about the level of commitment needed when participating in school-based reform projects. As previously mentioned, most external change agents actually spend little time with a particular school, and the nature of their work is often focused on only one aspect of education. A consultant comes into a school and conducts a workshop on discipline or curriculum development and then leaves. In contrast, as portrayed in chapters 3, 4, and 5, our work involves numerous areas of concern (e.g., interpersonal relationships, school governance, curriculum content, pedagogy, ideology). We have learned that substantive school reform requires extended periods of time (Watts and Castle, 1992):

> Today's meeting focused on the difficulty of substantive school reform. In the last couple of months it has seemed that several teachers were becoming hesitant about the number and types of new ideas and practices being suggested as part of this school's reform program. During this meeting we talked about risk-taking and the courage it takes to significantly reconceptualize the way in which we think about and practice education. After all, aside from demands to raise test scores or use more technology, there is not a great deal of support for the progressive pedagogy being considered in this school. At one point, Daniel had to remind the teachers that they were "in control" of what changes were to take place, and that not everything had to be implemented "yesterday." That is, the alterations being considered could be acted upon at a rate that seemed reasonable to the teachers. Ideas or values that seemed alien could be considered over a period of time, before judgments were made. (summary of field notes)

This meeting, and others like it, have indicated to us just how important it is to listen carefully to the teachers with whom we work, and to realize that it is they, and not we, who are taking the real risks imbedded in progressive school reform.

In fact, most schools do not initially share our visions of education and society. Many schools approach us because they express a desire to do something innovative or different, but have few ideas of what it is they want to do. In these situations, commitment suggests that time is taken to find common ground between the values and visions of the teachers and principal and our own. While many of the teachers and principals in these schools have, to some extent, bought into the conservative agenda, we have found that most teachers have a deep sense of caring and public service. We have consistently been impressed with practitioners' genuine desire to put the welfare of children before all other concerns. In our discussions with teachers and principals, most individuals agree that schools should be more interested in educating young people to help create a more compassionate and democratic society rather than merely serving as vocational training sites for industry. We have found many practitioners who are willing to let go of previously held values rooted in an industrial, technocratic ideology if given authoritative support to do so. As Grumet (1988) suggested over a decade ago, teachers deeply resonate to values imbedded in a more "womanist" pedagogy. We have learned that notions of caring and democracy are particularly useful as heuristic concepts in exploring with teachers and principals ways to reform interpersonal power relationships, the curriculum, and the types of educational experiences found within schools.

However, questions of commitment go beyond the amount of time needed to find common ground and see a project to its end. Since we often encourage teachers and principals to make progressive alterations in the education of their students, we feel committed to provide whatever support needed to defend these views and practices if challenged. This responsibility often requires us to assume the role of public advocate for the schools with which we work. This advocacy is particularly important during these decades of conservative restoration, as Finkelstein (1984: p. 273) noted,

> For the first time in the history of school reform, a deeply materialist consciousness seems to be overwhelming all other concerns. . . . Contemporary reformers seem to be recalling public education from its traditional utopian mission—to nurture a critical and committed citizenry that would . . . extend the workings of political democracy. . . . Americans, for the first time in a one-hundred-and-fifty-year history, seem ready to do ideological surgery on their public schools—cutting them away from the fate of social justice and political democracy completely and grafting them instead onto elite corporate, industrial, military, and cultural interests.

As previously mentioned, we have advocated for particular schools in their dealings with the state Department of Education, central administrations, unions, local school boards, and parent-teacher organizations. We also have assisted schools in locating and have written letters of support to funding agencies.

There are, of course, schools that want to work with us that may agree with our social and educational values in broad terms and for whom we have been public advocates, but wish or have little choice due to local or state "mandates" to continue pedagogical practices (e.g., punitive-based discipline, tracking, standardized testing, or textbook-based curriculum) that to us contradict our commitment to democratic education. Then there are those teachers who might be acting out (consciously or unconsciously) racist, sexist, or classist attitudes or perspectives. What should our reaction be to these situations? Should we continue to work with these schools or teachers when our involvement (especially in light of our willingness to serve as public advocates) may implicitly endorse practices that we believe do not serve the interests of or may even harm students? If we decide not to work with these schools, what does this decision suggest about our commitment to public education?

In exploring these questions, we have drawn from Glickman's (1998) reflections: The most important question to ask is, what is gained by not working in these schools or individuals? Unless our departure will cause a major disruption (which it won't), the objectionable practice(s) are almost certain to continue. Although our own reputation may be protected because people will not be able to say we support schools that condone such abhorrent practice(s), there seems little to gain from leaving such a situation. Perhaps we will find ways of altering the conditions that keep the practice(s) or attitude(s) entrenched. We have learned the value of being patient, raising questions, offering suggestions, articulating images of democratic pedagogy, trying to understand others' perspectives, experiencing obstacles, and looking for opportunities.

However, what if a school is doing harm to students, and our work is to no avail? Do we call a press conference and denounce what is going on? Would anyone from the press even come? Although there are given situations in which public repudiation is warranted (such as Kozol's [1967] account of the racist brutality he found in the Boston public schools), in most cases this does not seem like a particularly useful response. If little headway is being made to reform a given school, then at some point it seems logical to put our energies in other places. How do we know when this time comes?

As Glickman (1998) points out, much depends upon our own sense of hope. It makes sense to leave when we have lost hope that the teachers and principal are still interested in asking questions, reflecting on experiences, or examining possibilities. Notice that our decision is not based upon our hope that the school eventually does what we wish it would do. People who are moral, well informed, and thoughtful will often disagree with each other, and we view this disagreement as both useful and intelligent. Only when we lose hope in our abilities to generate an atmosphere in which we can learn from each other, does it seem time to leave a particular school. Making a commitment to assist teachers and principals in school-reform efforts suggests an obligation to "hang in there."

Is It Radical Enough?

During the last decade, there has been a growing recognition regarding the potential power of scholarly narrative. Educators and scholars have found that analytical portrayals of school reform provide vicarious experiences and thus insights that can be useful in other social locations. This book represents one contribution to this scholarship. Our purpose was to initiate and participate in a scholarly interchange of ideas. However, this purpose does not suggest that one should ignore issues of quality. Do the activities of these schools suggest that something significant was happening in them, or as previously stated, is it radical enough?

As Roemer (1991, p. 447) agues, too often school reform results in "change without difference." For example, does redistribution of power, authentic discourse among faculty, planning and implementing school or classroom-based curriculum, or using uniforms represent significant alterations in these schools? When has a school changed enough to be considered truly reformed? This is a particularly difficult question to answer for several reasons. First, the conventional popular measure of looking at children's test scores on standardized tests to determine the quality of school reform says little about the substance of the specific reforms. More importantly, these tests provide feedback on an extremely narrow range of intellectual ability and skill, ignoring a vast range of cognitive, social, and moral dimensions of educating children. Certain reforms, such as drill-and-skill instructional programs, may raise children's test scores but greatly limit young people's natural curiosity, thoughtfulness, and desire to learn. These types of instructional reform programs may also undermine teachers' ability to judge what is educationally worthwhile and intellectually stimulating. Reforms that result in short-term gains in standardized test scores may be implemented at the expense of teachers' and students' long-term intellectual and social growth. Second, it is impossible to divorce notions of significant reform from one's perspective. As Cuban (1990, p. 72) illustrated,

> A century-and-a-half ago tax-supported common schools took in boys and girls from cities and farms, as well as migrants and immigrants. . . . To some people these planned changes or reforms appeared to be progress toward a better fit between democracy and the schooling that children received. In the eyes of other observers, however, these changes were seen as efforts by an elite class to shape the beliefs, values, and behavior of children to meet the social and economic needs of those in power. In this view the innovations of nineteenth-century schooling are seen not as improvements but as impositions of the powerful upon the weak—as forms of social control. The judgment of whether a change is an improvement, then, rests in the mind of the beholder.

For some individuals, tracking is a progressive reform designed to help teachers individualize instruction, while for others it is a nefarious practice that undermines the self-confidence and efficacy of the vast majority of students. The types of changes that these schools have implemented obviously reflect our own subjective perspectives of progressive educational reform. It is a myth that schools can improve outside of an ideological context.

However, even if the criteria for worthwhile reforms can be determined, there is still the question of how much a school needs to change before these reforms are considered radical enough. As Deever (1996) argued, perhaps this is an inappropriate question. Substantive school-based reform is messy and time-consuming business. It cannot work in an atmosphere built upon a fast-food mentality. Schools are extremely complex institutions that are often irrational and contradictory in nature. The structural patterns and bureaucratic practices found in them have a long and entrenched history. In the initial stages of school-based reform, we must accept the fact that working within these structures is necessary. If significant change is instituted from within, then one must be prepared to accept the irrational and at times contradictory movement of this change. After all, a given school (and district) will not suddenly abolish the top-down flow of power, teachers will not abruptly become designers of school or classroom-based curriculum, parents will not suddenly become welcome partners in school affairs, students will not come to school one day to find they have an authentic voice over decisions that directly impact their educational lives, and politicians will not abruptly give up their control over what happens in education. The creative challenge of substantive school-based reform projects is not to articulate the ideal school, but rather to bring the mosaic of progressive pedagogical and social ideas into the everyday lives of educators, parents, and children. To look at a school and say, "Well, this isn't enough" misses the point. The more appropriate question is, "Does a given effort advance the educational and social principles of equity, community, social justice, intellectual engagement, and authentic human growth?" Although there may be signs that indicate a school is moving in a certain direction, there are no lines of demarcation that indicates a school has arrived. As Deever (1994, p. 9) states, "The whole question, 'Is this radical enough?' obliterates the points we [school reformers] should be considering." From this perspective it is the struggle rather than the result at any given time that is most important. It is the struggle, not any one particular product, that gives meaning to this work. However, it is important to note that the implementation of ideas and recognition of success is necessary. The continual generation of ideas and actions, that is, genuine educational reform, works best when a given school is able to build upon its achievements. Is it enough? The answer in truly dynamic schools will always be "no."

Reflective Scholarship

Finally, it is important to conclude this discussion with a reflection upon the work of this book, itself. As mentioned in chapter 2, its purpose was not to evaluate the effectiveness of our work, to measure our success, or to identify our strengths and weaknesses. Rather, it was to identify and portray the substance of our work and examine significant ideas and issues in relation to this work that others might find instructive. However, there is an obvious danger in conducting self-reflective studies. In particular, there is always the risk that the authors will conduct their analysis in ways that are self-serving. This potential for conducting a self-serving study might easily have influenced all aspects of our inquiry from taking observation notes, asking certain types of interview and follow-up questions, reviewing field notes, making decisions about what aspects of our work to portray, selecting the ideas and issues related to this portrayal, and generating the final analysis. This potential for self-interest is especially problematic when those who conduct the study authentically have confidence in what they do and who find their work personally and socially meaningful. Given this experience, one might ask, how likely are we to publically disclose our failings or analyze our work from an antagonistic perspective? This question becomes particularly important if there is a covert purpose to use this or other articles as a way to generate "business."

Unfortunately, we are not meta-cognitive enough to know for sure if this potential self-interest has corrupted the analytical portrayal of our work. We do know that our involvement in schools has never been initiated by knowledge obtained from any of the scholarly articles or papers we have written. All of our work, to date, has come to us through word of mouth, and our purpose for engaging in scholarly discourse is pedagogical, not financial. That is, we conducted this self-reflective study as a means to learn and grow from our work and to share what we have learned with, in this case, other scholars, teachers, school reformers, and educational leaders. We have found this process of self-study intellectually stimulating and challenging. Nevertheless, educators and scholars who wish to pursue this particular method of inquiry (and we strongly encourage others to do so), should take the issue of self-interest seriously, and recognize the embedded risks involved in such endeavors.

CONCLUSION

This book has portrayed work of the Harmony Education Center during the first twelve years of its existance. In particular, it has provided an analytical description of our efforts working in more than fifty schools throughout the United States, although special attention was paid to our efforts in five high-poverty schools during the latter half of the 1990s. Although our attention has shifted away from focusing most of our work in specific schools during the last four years (see *http://www.harmonyschool.org/* or *http://www.nsrfharmony.org/*), our resources are still concentrated on working with those individuals who are directly responsible for the education of our nation's young people.

Needless to say, the educational policies that have emerged from the Bush administration have made our work significantly more difficult. The extremely conservative (and what some might call reactionary) educational agenda of this administration has created a climate of fear and intimidation among our nation's teachers and administrators as well as their students. One does not have to be an educator to recognize that creating an atmosphere of anxiety and trepidation is not reflective of the ideal learning environment for our educators or their students. At the same time, Bush's international and tax policies have put the country's resources for education in a desperate situation. No Child Left Behind has (perhaps unintentionally) resulted in an underfunded mandate that conservatives use to express outrage when more progressive administrations have tried to require states to regulate their industries. The coalition between the traditional bourgeoisie, technical intelligentsia, fundamentalist

Christians, and "angry white men," is a force that is clearly impacting our schools in ways that make it difficult to help those educators who want to authentically and meaningfully educate children in ways that deepen and broaden our imperfect democracy. Although difficult, reform-leftist scholars would provide a crucial service to the nation if they would abandon what Hook (1975) referred to as an obsession with calls for revolutionary change of society as a whole, what he called the academic "cult of revolution." Instead, the focus of leftist scholarship would be more useful if it followed Dewey's (1920) recommendation and offered compelling social visions and discourses of specific critiques or reforms within particular spheres of society that would once again attract people (especially the electorate) and thus enlarge the current leftist coalition found within our society.

Although getting the society as a whole to move in a more progressive direction seems futile at times during this conservative era, during the more than twelve years in which the Harmony Education Center has worked with educators throughout the United States, we have been extremely impressed with their authentic desire to make life better for their students and to view the education of children as one way to make our society more authentically democratic, socially just, and inclusive. In spite of the current demands coming from the political sphere of our society to evaluate not only children's knowledge and learning but an entire school by the scores that students receive on a single test, tens of thousands of educators are still dedicated to teaching young people a curriculum that is responsive and meaningful to themselves and their pupils. There are also hundreds of progressive, grassroots educational organizations (in addition to HEC) dedicated to assisting educators in their work. This commitment, perhaps more than anything else, keeps our spirits and our enthusiasm alive during this period of unenlightened political leadership.

It is perhaps most appropriate to terminate this book by once again taking the historical perspective advocated by Dewey's pragmatism. As previously mentioned (see chapter 1), school reform (as well as other meaningful alterations of society) is not an "event." Schools will not change as a result of some monumental, revolutionary transformation of our entire society, but only through the diligent, hard work of conversations, imagination, planning, and reflection in specific locations with real people. School reform is a process, not a singular occurrence.

Given the influence of conservative ideology on many spheres (including education) within our society during the last quarter of a century, it is not difficult for progressive-thinking citizens and educators to become frustrated, discouraged, or even cynical about the possibility of improving our schools and society. However, there are two important points to keep in mind during these troublesome times. First, it is useful to view societal reform from a much longer historical perspective than one's own lifetime. Even with the increasingly rapid changes in technology, it is still very difficult to understand cultural shifts within a period of sixty to ninety years. Although the last twenty five or thirty years (and especially the last five years given the result of the 2000 and 2004 elections) have been dominated by a conservative ideology in the United States, when the quality of life in this country during the twentieth century is compared to life during the nineteenth or eighteenth centuries in terms of social justice, equity, democracy, environmental protection, prosperity, health care, education, and freedom; it is a bit easier to see the progressive nature of our society. In spite of the conservative restoration (and the extreme manifestation it has taken under the Bush administration), there are millions of progressive-thinking citizens working hard to make our society into a more social, liberal, and critical democracy.

Second, as previously mentioned, it is important to avoid placing too much emphasis on the results of any given effort at reform. That is, the meaning and authenticity of a given reform effort is best contextualized in the struggle rather than in the results of our efforts. If we focus on short-term success, then it is easy to see, given the current socio-political climate in our nation, why progressive-thinking citizens might easily become discouraged and withdraw into private life. However, if our sense of accomplishment and meaning lies in the struggles in which we choose to engage, rather than merely the end result of those struggles, then it is possible to develop the historical perspective needed to pass the struggle on to the next generation. It is this willingness to voluntarily struggle, even during difficult times, that best reflects what it means to work within a progressive tradition.

NOTES

CHAPTER 1

1. As Menand (2001) and Goodman (1995) note, there has been a renewed interest in American pragmatism during the last decade. Similar to many on the Left, we have found Dewey's alternate orientation to scholarship (1920) and social action (1946 [1929]) much more relevant to our goals than say, the tradition of Marxism. American pragmatism is attractive for many reasons. First, like Hegel, Darwin, and Marx, Dewey (1920) argued that our conception of the world should emerge primarily from the study of human and natural history. Most importantly, and similar to postmodernism, pragmatism rejects the notion of "Truth" with a capital "T." All ideas are human constructions and, as Nietzsche (1968) argues in many of his works, what we call truth is largely a matter of social, geographical, and historical location and personal biography. There are no fixed, eternal, or essential truths regarding human existence or the construction of culture, or what Rorty (1989) refers to as a "final vocabulary." Instead of seeking truth, Dewey suggested that we search for "warranted assertability," that is, ideas that enrich and deepen our existence over time and in light of human experience. Unlike postmodernists, Dewey recognized the contingent "truth" (with a small "t") embedded in the social contract that exists between people at any given time and location. Every social contract contains, what Foucault (1970) refers to as regimes of truth, or what others (e.g., Apple, 1996) refer to as "cultural capital," that is, ideas, values, knowledge, and ways of acting and being that are taken for granted as "truth." Some of these ideas are codified into laws, while many others are informal understandings such as "proper manners" (Elias, 1982). From a pragmatist perspective, human cultures are best viewed as temporary social contracts among people of unequal power who seek to influence what cultural capital is deemed most worthy and/or what "truths" govern society as a whole. In this way, pragmatism avoids the nihilism implied in much of the postmodern project. Although there are no ultimate, immutable values, structures, systems, or ideals upon which a given society should be based, we, as members of a given society, can tentatively (and to some degree arbitrarily) identify a multiplicity of values (e.g., prosperity, social justice, democracy, freedom, liberty), systems, and structures (e.g., the U.S. Constitution) that we use in the construction and modification of culture. These types of truth claims can be useful as long as they maintain their basic vulnerability and contingency (Rorty, 1989). In other words, the value of any idea is not rooted in its ability to mimic or "represent the world" in which we live, but rather lies ultimately in its usefulness in understanding our experiences and in living meaningful lives. From a pragmatist perspective, the truth of any idea ultimately lies in human experience. This rejection of universal and unchanging truths extends to our understanding of morality. Pragmatism forces us, as scholars and activists, to be highly skep-

tical of actions based on claims of moral righteousness. Great misery often comes from those who claim to represent some form of architectonic morality. For example, our commitment to the notion of democracy is not based upon its "moral superiority" over other forms of government, but rather upon its utility in allowing people with different public interests to tentatively resolve disputes over public policy without resorting to armed conflict. There is nothing "moral" about democracy, it is just a more compelling basis for establishing a polity over other possibilities of which we are currently or historically aware. Similarly, we are not advocates of a society that is committed to social or economic justice because it is "moral," but rather, because it is in the self-interest of society (more stability, greater contentment among citizens) as a whole to avoid having significant numbers of its citizens oppressed by poverty, or suffer from discrimination, or live without hope and opportunities. Pragmatists recognize the importance of the continued struggle to balance competing ideas and values in the reform of society. Pragmatists are thus not nihilists but rather value pluralists who recognize that the most difficult task of the scholar or reformer is not to advocate for a particular social value such as democracy, freedom, social control, prosperity, liberty, empowerment, or social and economic justice, but rather to address the difficulty of balancing competing values that are all needed in order to develop the "good" society (Galston, 2002).

2. "Otherization" refers to identification and degradation of a subgroup of the total population as outside the circle of moral obligation. Industrial workers at the beginning of the industrial revolution, Jews in many parts of Europe prior to the end of World War II, black South Africans under apartheid, and persons of color prior to the Civil Rights legislation in the United States are just a few of many obvious examples of people who have been "otherized" in feudal and capitalist societies. In addition, the otherization of people also occurred in twentieth-century, Marxist-inspired states. The clearest illustration is the transformation of the term *bourgeois* that occurred at the end of the nineteenth century throughout much of Europe. Prior to this time, *bourgeois* simply identified merchants. However, by 1900, and as a result of Marxist politics, this term identified a group of people who did not have a right to exist in a "just" society. Within the twentieth-century Marxist experiments, this category eventually encompassed anyone who disagreed with those in power (Courtois et al., 1999). It is also worthy to note the distinction between social marginalization and otherization. Although functioning democracies will often marginalize "political heretics"—that is, people who vocalize aberrant social, psychological, economic, and political views—it will not, if truly democratic, otherize (i.e., de-humanize, criminalize, physically ostracize) individuals who espouse these ideas. For example, most modernist states currently do not otherize overt racists, but have, since World War II, established a system of informal condemnation that limits or hinders racists from publicly espousing their ideas and have passed laws that prevent them from acting on their beliefs.

3. As we have discussed in much greater detail elsewhere, Marx's analysis of capitalism was deeply flawed (e.g., Goodman and Holloway, 2000; Gouldner, 1979, 1980; Lovell, 1988). However, reform leftists do agree with Marx in his assertion that inequities are built into the economics of capitalism. However, simply stating that there are inequalities built into capitalism does not help us as a polity unless one has a viable and demonstratively better alternative vision of society. Unfortunately, as a theory upon which to build alternative economic, political, and/or social systems, struc-

tures, and societies, Marxism has shown itself, as illustrated by the numerous twentieth-century experiments, to be a dismal failure. In particular, the inability of Marxist-
Leninist-inspired nations to tolerate a public "loyal opposition" and thus establish a
democratic polity to solve the problem of scarcity and create prosperous economies; or
to avoid degenerating into brutal totalitarian states (e.g., Avrich, 1970; Burgler, 1990;
Courtois et al., 1999; Dolot, 1985; Hosking, 1985; Kornai, 1992; Lazzerini, 1999;
Meredith, 2002; Pipes, 1990, 1995; Soltys, 1997; Tang et al., 2000; Wlodzimierz and
Laski, 1989) suggest that Marxism/Leninism offers few ideas that are of genuine value
in building a more humane society. Given our rejection of all inferences that our analysis or activities should be based upon utopianism, we agree with those cultural critics
and social theorists (e.g., Aronson, 1995; Barber, 1998; Blank, 1997; Darby, 1996;
Dewey, 1946 (1929); Fraser, 1997; Gilbert and Gilbert, 1989; Hawken et al., 1999;
Miller, 1989; Rawls, 2001; Rorty, 1998; Sen, 2000; 1984; Sunstein, 1997) who argue
that we should diligently focus our energies toward building a critical, social, liberal
democracy (that will be discussed later in this chapter) until a feasible alternative is
articulated in a compelling manner.

4. The movement of radical leftists into university life should come as no surprise.
As Gouldner (1979) and others (e.g., Konrád and Szelenyi, 1979; Kornai, 1992) have
clearly examined, in spite of Marx's claim that socialism was the intrinsic consciousness of the industrial working class, revolutionary Marxist-Leninist philosophy has
always been much more attractive to intellectuals than industrial workers. None of the
twentieth-century experiments represent a situation where the industrial working class
actually assumed state power. To the contrary, each experiment was conceptualized,
initiated, and led by members of the intellectual and intellegentsia classes of these societies. These Marxist-inspired experiments represented dictatorships of these classes
rather than the "dictatorship of the proletariat" as suggested by Marx. It is not uncommon within academia for a Marxist scholar to respond to criticism of this intellectual
discourse by saying the critic just "doesn't understand" the complexities of Marx's (or
his disciples') thought. One must question just how inherent communism is to the
industrial working class if one needs to be an intellectual, that is, if it takes years of
studying complex economic and political theories, to understand it.

5. Perhaps the most obvious example of these coalitions can be found within the
political sphere of the United States, namely, the two most powerful political parties.
Currently, the Republican Party represents an uneasy coalition made up primarily of
bourgeoisie, evangelical Christians, Cuban Hispanics, and members of the technical
intelligentsia classes, while the Democratic Party reflects a coalition of people most
commonly associated with industrial workers (unions); the elderly, intellectuals
(including visual and performing artists); African, Asian, Italian, Irish, and Jewish
Americans; women; and a significant portion of the intelligentsia. Of course, there are
classes that are not part of these coalitions, such as those who live in poverty, and children under the age of 18.

6. Reformists are particularly attentive to the "politics of size." As an organization
(e.g., business, school) grows and thus its policies directly impact more people's lives,
it needs to come under closer public scrutiny. A small business, therefore, should have
far fewer governmental restrictions imposed upon it compared to larger corporations.
Reformists are particularly sensitive to the possibilities and problems that emerge due,
in part, to the growth in a culture's population. From a reformist perspective, many of

the problems associated with capitalist relations of production are more fundamentally associated to the politics of size. Recognition of these politics has been a driving force behind the "small schools" movement in the United States (e.g., Ayers, Klonsky, and Lyon, 2000).

7. For the purpose of this book, solving the problem of scarcity refers to a level of production and distribution in which a society has the capability to produce enough food, housing, clothing, basic medical care, education, and some leisure time for each citizen. Prosperity goes beyond this standard of living and includes providing citizens with significant leisure time, disposable income, and a plethora of goods and services that one can purchase to make life more comfortable and rewarding.

8. Rawls (2001) makes an excellent point where he states that even the benefits (e.g., wealth, power, privileges) that emerge directly from our talents are ultimately arbitrary and contingent. For example, those who were talented in hunting and skinning game would be likely to gain power in preagricultural societies, but those talents are not particularly useful in modern technological societies. From a reform-leftist perspective, within all cultures there are always personal characteristics, structures, and systems of power that will benefit some and not other members of that society. Since the former group's "success" is arbitrary and contingent, in part, upon these characteristics, structures, and systems of power, it is only socially just to have a portion of their wealth redistributed for the purpose of creating opportunities and protecting basic necessities and rights for those individuals who, for whatever reason, have a difficult time being successful under these same characteristics, structures, and systems.

9. As currently used (i.e., to support school choice for low-income students in urban centers with a record of poor schooling), many within the African American class support the voucher movement. These individuals want to help those African American parents who desire a better education for their children than can be found in the public domain and who do not have the wealth to do so privately (Howell et al., 2002).

10. There are many scholars who have cogently articulated such a vision or who have thoughtfully critiqued the conservative educational agenda, but these have emerged almost exclusively within the U.S. academic discourse. Even works that one might think would attract public attention, such as Berlinger and Biddle's (1995) well-researched and clearly written condemnation of the conservative agenda, have failed to do so.

11. There are many reasons to focus our attention on those who work in schools. Although recent actions by state and federal governments attempt to control what and how teachers and administrators teach and assess student learning, schools are still, to some degree, "loosely coupled" institutions (e.g., Meyer and Rowan, 1978). As a result, teachers and others who work directly with children are often able to carve out small "free spaces" (Wood, 1992) within which they can work meaningfully with children despite pressure to make schooling more like an assembly line process of production. However, teachers, administrators, and others working directly with children need significant support, such as provided by the Harmony Education Center and other similar organizations, in creating these "free spaces" and then utilizing these spaces for socially conscious and existentially meaningful educational activities.

CHAPTER 2

1. HEC recently became the "home" for the National School Reform Faculty. As a result of this association, ideas, values, and structure of this expanded HEC is going through a period of particularly deep reflection and potentially significant changes in its governance structure.

2. The denigration of merchants was also due in part to antisemitism. Due to restrictions on owning land to farm, joining professions, and becoming craftsmen, many Jews were forced into the fields of banking, trading, shipping, selling, and international commerce.

CHAPTER 4

1. Student Leadership Teams (SLTs) were created with representatives from each classroom. Unlike "student councils" that plan parties and bake sales, the purpose of the SLTs was similar to SGs. Students chose topics to study (with the assistance of an adult volunteer) and made proposals to improve the school. All proposals from the SLTs go directly to the LT in each school for consideration in the same way as proposals from the other SGs. If SLT proposals did not achieve consensus in the LT, then a dialogue was initiated to work out differences until it could obtain consensus by both the LT and the faculty as a whole.

2. In each school, we have had to carefully monitor compliance to these standards of interaction during meetings and when informed of noncompliance by others. In almost every case, we have assumed the responsibility for initially demonstrating the way "gentle reminders" can be expressed. Once we became aware of an instance of noncompliance, we brought it to the attention of all concerned so that over the course of the first year, these standards were internalized by most faculty.

REFERENCES

Allington, R. (2002). *Big brother and the national reading curriculum: How ideology trumped evidence*. Portsmouth, NH: Heinemann Press.

Allman, P. (2001). *Critical education against global capitalism: Karl Marx and revolutionary critical education*. Westport, CT: Bergin & Garvey.

Althusser, L. (1972). *Lenin and philosophy, and other essays*. New York: Monthly Review Press.

Ambrose, S. (1971). *Rise to globalism: American foreign policy since 1938*. Baltimore, MD: Penguin Books, Inc.

Andersen, R. (1995). *Consumer culture and tv programming*. Boulder, CO: Westview Press.

Anderson, G. (1990). Toward a critical constructivist approach to school administration: Invisibility, legitimization, and the study of non-events. *Educational Administration Quarterly*, 26 (1), 38–59.

Anderson, G. (1998). Toward authentic participation: Deconstructing the discourses of participatory reforms in education. *American Educational Research Journal*, 35 (4), 571–603.

Anderson, G. and Grinberg, J. (1998). Educational administration as a disciplinary practice: Appropriating Foucault's view of power, discourse, and method. *Educational Administration Quarterly*, 34 (3), 329–353.

Anyon, J. (1997). *Ghetto schooling: A political economy of urban educational reform* . New York: Teachers College Press.

Apple, M. (1986). *Teachers and texts: A political economy of class and gender relations in education*. London: Routledge & Kegan Paul.

Apple, M. (1996). *Cultural politics and education*. New York: Teachers College Press.

Apple, M. (2001). *Educating the "right" way: Markets, standards, God, and inequality*. New York: Routledge/Falmer Press.

Apple, M. & Teitelbaum, K. (1986). Are teachers losing control of their skills and curriculum? *Journal of Curriculum Studies*, 18 (2), 177–184.

Aronowitz, S. (1992). *The politics of identity*. New York: Routledge Press.

Aronson, R. (1992). After communism. *Rethinking Marxism*, 5 (2), 23–44.

Aronson, R. (1995). *After Marxism*. New York: Guilford Press.

Armstrong, T. (2000). *Multiple intelligences in the classroom*. Alexandria, VA: Association for Supervision and Curriculum.

Avrich, P. (1970). *Kronstadt 1921*. Princeton, NJ: Princeton University Press.

Ayers, W., Klonsky, M., & Lyon, G. (2000). *A simple justice: The challenge of small schools*. New York: Teachers College Press.

Baldwin, J. (1997). *The scholastic culture in the Middle Ages, 1000–1300*. Prospect Heights, IL: Waveland Press.

Banaszak, L. (1996). *Why movements succeed or fail: Opportunity, culture, and the struggle for woman suffrage.* Princeton, NJ: Princeton University Press.

Banathy, B. (1992). *Systems design of education: A journey to create the future.* Englewood Cliffs, NJ: Educational Technology Press.

Barber, B. (1992). *An aristocracy of everyone: The politics of education and the future of America.* New York: Oxford University Press.

Barber, B (1995). *Jihad vs. Mcworld: How globalism and tribalism are reshaping the world.* New York: Times Books.

Barber, B. (1998). *A place for us: How to make society civil and democracy strong.* New York: Hill & Wang Press.

Barker, J. (1993). Tightening the iron cage: Coercive control in self-managing teams. *Administrative Science Quarterly,* 38 (3), 408–437.

Barth, R. (1990). *Improving schools from within: Teachers, parents, and principals can make a difference.* San Francisco: Jossey-Bass.

Bates, S. (1993). *Battleground: One mother's crusade, the religious right, and the struggle for control of our classrooms.* New York: Poseidon Press.

Beare, H. (1993). Different ways of viewing school-site councils: Whose paradigm is in use here? In H. Beare & W. Boyd (Eds.), *Restructuring schools: An international perspective on the movement to transform the control and performance of schools,* pp. 200–217. London: Falmer Press.

Bell, D. (1973). *The coming of the post-industrial society: A venture in social forecasting.* New York: Basic Books.

Bellah, R., Madsen, R., Sullivan, W., & Tipton, S. (1985). *Habits of the heart: Individualism and commitment in American life.* Berkeley, CA: University of California Press.

Bennett, W. (1992). *The de-valuing of America: The fight for our culture and our children.* New York: Summit Books.

Berlinger, D. & Biddle, B. (1995). *The manufactured crisis: Myths, fraud, and the attack on America's public schools.* Reading, MA: Addison-Wesley.

Binder, A. (2002). *Contentious curricula: Afrocentrism and creationism in American public schools.* Princeton, NJ: Princeton University Press.

Bintz, W. (1995). *Curriculum and curriculum development as inquiry.* Bloomington, IN: Indiana University Dissertation.

Black, D. (1989). *Sociological justice.* New York: Oxford University Press.

Blank, R. (1997). *It takes a nation: A new agenda for fighting poverty.* Princeton, NJ: Princeton University Press.

Blase, J. (1998, April). *The micropolitics of educational change.* Paper presented at the annual American Educational Research Association meeting.

Blase, J. & Anderson, G. (1995). *The micropolitics of educational leadership: From control to empowerment.* New York: Teachers College Press.

Blau, J. (1999). *Illusions of prosperity: America's working families in an age of economic insecurity.* New York: Oxford University Press.

Bloom, L. (1992). How can we know the dancer from the dance: Discourses of the self-body. *Human Studies,* 15 (3), 313–334.

Bloom, L. (2004, April). *Poverty, welfare, and education in the U.S.* Oral presentation at the American Educational Research Association meeting.

Bobbitt, F. (1924). *How to make a curriculum.* Boston: Houghton Mifflin.

Bodnar, J. (1996). *Bonds of affection*. Princeton, NJ: Princeton University Press.

Brimelow, P. (2003). *The worm in the apple: How the Teacher unions are destroying American education*. New York: Harper Collins.

Brock, D. (2001). *Blinded by the right: The conscience of an ex-conservative*. New York: Crown Press.

Brosio, R. (2004). Essay review: Critical education against global capitalism: Karl Marx and revolutionary critical education. *Educational Studies*, 34 (4), 446–464.

Buber, M. (1958). *I and thou*. New York: Scribner.

Buchanan, P. (2002). *The death of the West: How dying populations and immigrant invasions imperil our country and civilization*. New York: Thomas Dunne Books.

Buckmaster, H. (1992). *Let my people go: The story of the underground railroad and the growth of the abolition movement*. Columbia: University of South Carolina Press.

Buechler, S. (2000). *Social movements in advanced capitalism: The political economy cultural construction of social activism*. New York: Oxford University Press.

Bullough, R. & Gitlin, A. (1985). Schooling and change: A view from the lower rung. *Teachers College Record*, 87 (2), 219–237.

Bullough, R. & Gitlin, A. (1995). *Becoming a student of teaching: Methodologies for exploring self and school context*. New York: Garland Press.

Burgler, R. (1990). *The eyes of the pineapple: Revolutionary intellectuals and the terror in democratic Kampuchea*. Fort Lauderdale, FL: Verlag Breitenbach Press.

Campbell, J. & Neill, S. (1994). *Curriculum at stage one: Teacher commitment and policy failure*. Harlow, UK: Longman Press.

Campbell J. & Southworth, G. (1990, April). *Rethinking collegiality: Teachers' views*. Paper presented at the annual American Educational Research Association meeting, Boston.

Casner-Lotto, J. (1988). Expanding the teacher's role: Hammond's school improvement process. *Phi Delta Kappan*, 69 (5), 349–353.

Cassirer, E. (1981). *Kant's life and thought*. New Haven: Yale University Press.

Chapman, J. & Boyd, W. (1986). Decentralization, devolution and the school principal: Australian lessons on statewide educational reform. *Educational Administration Quarterly*, 22 (4), 28–58.

Charters, W. (1924). *Curriculum construction*. New York: Macmillan.

Chubb, J. & Moe, T. (1990). *Politics, markets, and America's schools*. Washington, DC: The Brookings Institute.

Cohen, G. (1995). *Self-ownership, freedom, and equality*. Cambridge, UK: Cambridge University Press.

Comer, J., Haynes, N., Joyner, E., Ben-Avie, M. (1996). *Rallying the whole village: The Comer Process for reforming education*. New York: Teachers College Press.

Courtois, S., Werth, N., Panne, J., Paczkowski, A., Bartosek, K., & Margolin, J. (1999). *The black book of communism: Crimes, terror, repression*. Cambridge, MA: Harvard University Press.

Crawford, J. (1991). *Bilingual education: History, politics, theory, and practice*. Los Angeles: Bilingual Educational Services.

Crawford, J. (1992). *Hold your tongue: Bilingualism and the politics of English only*. Reading, MA : Addison-Wesley Press.

Crawford, J. (2000). *At war with diversity: U.S. language policy in an age of anxiety*. Buffalo, NY: Multilingual Matters.

Cuban, L. (1990). A fundamental puzzle of school reform. In A. Lieberman (Ed.), *Schools as collaborative cultures: Creating the future now*. New York: Falmer Press.

Cubberley, E. (1916). *Public school administration*. Boston: Houghton Mifflin & Co.

Cumming, R. (1969). *Human nature and history: A study of the development of liberal political thought*. Chicago: University of Chicago Press.

Cummings, S. (1998). *The dixification of America: The American odyssey into the conservative economic trap*. Westport, CT: Praeger Press.

Damico, A. (1978). *Individuality and community: The social and political thought of John Dewey*. Gainesville, FL: University of Florida Press.

Darby, M. (1996). *Reducing poverty in America: Views and approaches*. Thousand Oaks, CA: Sage Publications.

Darling-Hammond, L. (1997). *The right to learn: A blueprint for creating schools that work*. San Francisco: Jossey-Bass.

Deever, B. (1996). Is this radical enough? Curriculum reform, change, and the language of probability. *Interchange* 27 (3–4), 251–260.

DeLue, S. (1989). *Political obligation in a liberal state*. Albany: State University of New York Press.

Dewey, J. (1920). *Reconstruction in philosophy*. New York: Holt & Co.

Dewey, J. (1927). *The public and its problems*. New York: Henry Holt.

Dewey, J. (1930). *Individualism old and new*. New York: Minton, Balch & Co.

Dewey, J. (1946 [1929]). *The problems of men*. New York: Philosophical Library.

Dewey, J. (1966 [1916]). *Democracy and education: An introduction to the philosophy of education*. New York: The Free Press.

Dewey, J. (1976 [1938]). *Experience and education*. New York: Collier Books.

Doerr, E. (1996). *The case against school vouchers*. Amherst, NY: Prometheus Books.

Dolot, M. (1985). *Execution by hunger: The hidden holocaust*. New York: W.W. Norton Press.

Dow, P. (1991). *Schoolhouse politics: Lessons from the Sputnik era*. Cambridge, MA: Harvard University Press.

Dreyfus, H. & Rabinow, P. (1983). *Michel Foucault: Beyond structuralism and hermeneutics*. Chicago: University of Chicago Press.

Duby, G. (1968). *Rural economy and country life in the medieval West*. Columbia, SC: University of South Carolina Press.

Duby, G. (1980). *The three orders: Feudal society imagined*. Chicago: University of Chicago Press.

Duffy, G., Roehler, L., & Putman, J. (1987). Putting the teacher in control: Basal reading textbooks and instructional decision making. *Elementary School Journal*, 87 (3), 359–366.

Dunayevskaya, R. (1992). *The Marxist-humanist theory of state-capitalism: Selected writings*. Chicago: News & Letters Press.

Durham, M. & Kellner, D. (2001). *Media and cultural studies*. Malden, MA: Blackwell Publishers.

Easton, N. (2000). *Gang of five: Leaders at the center of the conservative crusade*. New York: Simon & Schuster.

Edwards, R. (1979). *Contested terrain*. New York: Basic Books.

Elbaum, M. (2002). *Revolution in the air: Sixties radicals turn to Lenin, Mao and Che*. New York: Verso.

Elias, N. (1982). *The history of manners: The civilizing process*, vol. 1. New York: Pantheon Books.

Ellsberg, D. (2002). *Secrets: A memoir of Vietnam and the Pentagon papers.* New York: Viking Press.

Elmore, R. (1990). *Restructuring schools: The next generation of educational reform.* San Francisco: Jossey-Bass.

Engles, F. (1958 [1845]). *The condition of the working class in England.* Oxford, UK: Basil Blackwell Press.

Erickson, F. (1986). Qualitative research on teaching. In M. Wittrock (Ed.), *Handbook of research on teaching*, 119–161. New York: Macmillan.

Fashola, O. & Slavin, R. (1998). Schoolwide reform models: What works? *Phi Delta Kappan*, 79 (5), 370–379.

Fernández, D. (2000). *Cuba and the politics of passion.* Austin: University of Texas Press.

Finkelstein, B. (1984). Education and the retreat from democracy in the United States: 1979–198?. *Teachers College Record*, 86 (2), 273–282.

Finn, C. & Clements, S. (1989). *Reconnoitering Chicago's school reform efforts: Some early impressions.* Washington, DC: the Educational Excellence Network.

Finn, C., Ravitch, D., & Fancher, R. (1984). *Against mediocrity: The humanities in America's high schools.* New York: Holmes & Meier.

Foucault, M. (1970). *The order of things.* New York: Random House.

Fox, S. (1986). *The American conservation movement: John Muir and his legacy.* Madison, WI: University of Wisconsin Press.

Fraser J. (1999). *Between church and state: Religion and public education in a multicultural America.* New York: St. Martin's Press.

Fraser, N. (1997). *Justice interruptus: Critical reflections on the "postsocialist" condition.* New York: Routledge Press.

Freire, P. (1993). Pedagogy of the oppressed. New York: Continuum Books.

Friedman, T. (1999). *The Lexus and the olive tree: Understanding globalization.* New York: Farrar, Straus & Giroux.

Fromm, E. (1956). *The art of loving.* New York: Harper & Row.

Frye, M. (1983). *The politics of reality: Essays in feminist theory.* Trumansburg, NY: Crossing Press.

Frymier, J. (1987). Bureaucracy and the neutering of teachers. *Phi Delta Kappan*, 69 (9), 9–14.

Fullan, M. (1993). *Change forces: Probing the depths of educational reform.* London: Falmer Press.

Galbraith, J. (1958). *The affluent society.* Boston: Houghton Mifflin.

Galbraith, J. (1987). *Economics in perspective: A critical history.* Boston: Houghton Mifflin.

Galston, W. (2002). *Liberal pluralism: The implications of value pluralism for political theory and practice.* New York: Cambridge University Press.

Gardner, H. (1999). *Intelligence reframed: Multiple intelligences for the 21st century.* New York: Basic Books.

Garten, J. (2001). *The mind of the C.E.O.* New York: Basic Books.

Gay, P. (1979 [1952]). *The dilemma of democratic socialism: Eduard Bernstein's challenge to Marx .* New York: Octagon Books.

Gaylin, W. & Jennings, B. (1996). *The perversion of autonomy: The proper uses of coercion and constraints in a liberal society.* New York: The Free Press.

Gee, J. (1990). *Social linguistics and literacies: Ideology in discourses*. New York: Falmer Press.

Giddens, A. (2003). *The progressive manifesto: New ideas for the centre-left*. Cambridge, UK: Polity Press.

Gilbert, N. & Gilbert, B. (1989). *The enabling state: Modern welfare capitalism in America*. New York: Oxford University Press.

Giroux, H. (1995). Language, difference, and curriculum theory: Beyond the politics of clarity. In P. McLaren & J. Giarelli (Eds.), *Critical theory and educational research*. Albany: State University of New York Press, 23–38.

Giroux, H. (1999). *Corporate culture and the attack on higher education and public schooling*. Bloomington, IN: Phi Delta Kappa.

Gitlin, A. (1983). School structure, teachers' work and reproduction. In M. Apple & L. Weiss (Eds.), *Ideology and practice in education*. Philadelphia: Temple University Press, 193–212.

Gitlin, A. (1997). *Collaboration and progressive school reform*. Paper presented at the annual American Educational Research Association meeting.

Gitlin, A. & Margonis, F. (1995). The political aspect of reform: Teacher resistance as good sense. *American Journal of Education*, 103, 377–405.

Gitlin, T. (1987). *The sixties: Years of hope, days of rage*. New York: Bantam Books.

Glaser, G. & Strauss, A. (1975). *The discovery of grounded theory: Strategies for qualitative research*. Chicago: Aldine Press.

Glickman, C. (1993). *Renewing America's schools: A guide for school-based action*. San Francisco: Jossey-Bass Press.

Glickman, C. (1998). *Revolutionizing America's schools*. San Francisco: Jossey-Bass.

Goodman, J. (1986). Teaching preservice teachers a critical approach to curriculum design: A descriptive account. *Curriculum Inquiry*, 16 (2), 179–201.

Goodman, J. (1988). The disenfranchisement of elementary teachers and strategies for resistance. *Journal of Curriculum and Supervision*, 3 (3), 201–220.

Goodman, J. (1991). Redirecting sexuality education for young adolescents. *Curriculum and Teaching*, 6 (1), 12–22.

Goodman, J. (1992). *Elementary schooling for critical democracy*. Albany: State University of New York Press. *International Journal of Leadership in Education: Theory and Practice*, 4 (1), 67–86.

Goodman, J., Baron, D., Belcher, M., Hastings-Heinz, U., & James, J. (1994). Towards a comprehensive understanding of service education: Reflections from an exploratory action research project. *Research in Middle Level Education*, 18 (1), 39–63.

Goodman, J. & Holloway, L. (2000, October). *Dewey or Marx: Which way for leftist educators and scholars?* Paper presented at the annual Curriculum and Pedagogy conference.

Goodman, J. & Kuzmic, J. (1997). Bringing a progressive pedagogy to conventional schools: Theoretical and practical implications from Harmony. *Theory into Practice*, 36 (2), 79–86.

Goodman, P. (1964). *Compulsory mis-education*. New York: Vintage Books.

Goodman, R. (1995). *Pragmatism: A contemporary reader*. New York: Routledge Press.

Gourley, C. (1999). *Good girl work: Factories, sweatshops, and how women changed their role in the American workforce*. Brookfield, CT: Millbrook Press.

Gottlieb, R. (2005). *Forcing the spring: The transformation of the American environmental movement.* Washington, DC: Island Press.

Gouldner, A. (1979). *The future of intellectuals and the rise of the new class: A frame of reference, theses, conjectures, arguments, and an historical perspective on the role of intellectuals and intelligentsia in the international class contest of the modern era.* New York: The Seabury Press.

Gouldner, A. (1980). *The two Marxisms: Contradictions and anomalies in the development of theory.* New York: The Seabury Press.

Gramsci, A. (1971). *Selections from the prison notebooks of Antonio Gramsci.* New York: International Press.

Grumet, M. (1988). *Bitter milk: Women and teaching.* Amherst: University of Massachusetts Press.

Habermas, J. (1975). *Legitimation crisis.* Boston: Beacon Press.

Habermas, J. (1994). "Struggles for recognition in the democratic constitutional state." In C. Taylor (Ed.), *Multiculturalism: Examining the politics of recognition.* Princeton, NJ: Princeton University Press.

Hamann, J. (1992). *Contexts and processes for effective school change: Case study of an external change agent.* Paper presented at the annual American Educational Research Association meeting.

Hargreaves, A. (1994). *Changing times: Teachers' work and culture in the postmodern age.* New York: Teacher College Press.

Haskins, C. (1972 [1923]). *The rise of the universities.* Ithaca, NY: Cornell University Press.

Hatch, T. (1998). The differences in theory that matter in the practice of school improvement. *American Educational Research Journal,* 35 (1), 3–31.

Hawken, P., Lovins, A., & Hunter-Lovins, L. (1999). *Natural capitalism: Creating the next industrial revolution.* Boston: Little, Brown & Co.

Hay, G. (2001). *The early middle ages.* San Diego, CA: Greenhaven Press.

Hegel, G. (1942 [1821]). *Philosphy of right.* Oxford, UK: Clarendon Press.

Heilman, E. & Goodman, J. (1996). Teaching gender identity in high school. *The High School Journal,* 79 (3), 249–261.

Herman, J. & Golan, S. (1993). The effects of standardized testing on teaching and schools. *Educational-Measurement: Issues-and-Practice,* 12 (4), 20–25, 41–42.

Himmelberg, R. (1994). *The rise of big business and the beginnings of antitrust and railroad regulation, 1870–1900.* New York: Garland Press.

Hirsch, E.D. (1988). *Cultural literacy: What every American needs to know.* New York: Vintage Books.

Hobson, J. (1900). *The economics of distribution.* New York: Macmillan Co.

Hobson, J. (1920). *Taxation in the new state.* New York: Harcourt, Brace, & Howe.

Hobson, J. (1949 [1894]). *The evolution of modern capitalism: A study of machine production.* New York: Macmillan Co.

Hobson, J. (1971 [1902]). *Imperialism: A study.* Ann Arbor: University of Michigan Press.

Hollingsworth, S. (1997). *International action research: A casebook for educational reform.* Washington, DC: Falmer Press.

Holt, J. (1967). *How children learn.* New York: Pitman Publishing Corp.

Holton, R. (1985). *The transition from feudalism to capitalism.* New York: St. Martin's Press.

Hook, S. (1975). *Revolution, reform, and social justice: Studies in the theory and practice of Marxism*. New York: New York University Press.

Hosking, G. (1985). *The first socialist society: A history of the Soviet Union from within*. Cambridge, MA: Harvard University Press.

Howell, W., Peterson, P., Wolf, P., & Campbell, D. (2002). *The education gap: Vouchers and urban schools*. Washington, DC: Brookings Institution Press.

Huber, R. (1971). *The American idea of success*. New York: McGraw-Hill.

Huizinga, J. (1967). *The waning of the middle ages*. New York: St. Martin's Press.

Hunt, A. (1992). Can Marxism survive? *Rethinking Marxism*, 5 (2), 45–63.

Hunter, J. (1991). *Culture wars: The struggle to define America*. New York: Basic Books.

Isserman, M. & Kazin, M. (2000). *America divided: The civil war of the 1960s*. New York: Oxford University Press.

Jay, M. (1973). *The dialectic imagination: A history of the Frankfurt school and the institute of social research*. Boston: Little Brown & Co.

Kant, I. (1959 [1785]). *Foundations of the metaphysics of morals*. Indianapolis: Bobbs-Merrill.

Kaplan, G. (1994). Shotgun wedding: Notes on public education's encounter with the new Christian right. *Phi Delta Kappan*, 75 (9), k1–k12.

Katz, M. (1968). *The irony of early school reform: Educational innovation in mid-nineteenth century Massachusetts*. Cambridge: Harvard University Press.

Katz, M. (1995). *Improving poor people: The welfare state, the "underclass," and urban schools as history*. Princeton, NJ: Princeton University Press.

Kessler-Harris, A. (2001). *In pursuit of equity: Women, men, and the quest for economic citizenship in twentieth-century America*. New York: Oxford University Press.

Keynes, J. (1926). *The end of laissez-faire*. London: L. & Virginia Woolf Publishers.

Klein, F. (1989). *Curriculum reform in the elementary school: Creating your own agenda*. New York: Teachers College Press.

Kloppenberg, J. (1986). *Uncertain victory: Social democracy and progressivism in European and American thought, 1870–1920*. New York: Oxford University Press.

Knapp, M. & Adelman, N. (1995). *Teaching for meaning in high-poverty classrooms*. New York: Teachers College Press.

Kohl, H. (1967). *36 children*. New York: New American Library.

Kohn, A. (2000). *The case against standardized testing: Raising the scores, ruining the schools*. Portsmouth, NH: Heinemann.

Konrád, G. & Szelenyi, I. (1979). *The intellectuals on the road to class power*. New York: Harcourt Brace Jovanovich.

Kornai, J. (1992). *The socialist system: The political economy of communism*. Princeton, NJ: Princeton University Press.

Korostoff, M., Beck, L., & Gibb, S. (1998, April). *Supporting school-based reform: Lessons from the work of the California Center for School Restructuring*. Paper presented at the annual American Educational Research Association meeting.

Korten, D. (1998). *The post-corporate world: Life after capitalism*. San Francisco: Berrett-Koehler Press.

Kozol, J. (1967). *Death at an early age: The destruction of the hearts and minds of negro children in the Boston public schools*. Boston: Houghton Mifflin.

Kozol, J. (1992). *Savage inequalities: Children in America's schools*. New York: Harper.

Kurlansky, M. (2004). *1968: The year that rocked the world*. New York: Ballantine Books.

Kuzmic, J. (1990). *Toward a practice informed theory of critical pedagogy: Individualism, community, and democratic schooling.* Bloomington: Indiana University Dissertation.

Lachmann, R. (2000). *Capitalist in spite of themselves: Elite conflict and economic transitions in early modern Europe.* New York: Oxford University Press.

Ladson-Billings, G. (1994). *The dreamkeepers: Successful teachers of African American children.* San Francisco: Jossey-Bass Publishers.

Lasch, C. (1978). *The culture of narcissism: American life in an age of diminishing expectations.* New York: W.W. Norton.

Lather, P. (1986). Research as praxis. *Harvard Educational Review,* 56(3): 257–277.

Lawson, N. & Sherlock, N. (2001). *The progressive century: The future of the centre-left in Britain.* New York: Palgrave Books.

Lazzerini, E. (1999). *The Chinese revolution.* Westport, CT: Greenwood Press.

Le Blanc, P. (1999). *A short history of the U.S. working class: From colonial times to the twenty-first century.* Amherst, NY: Humanity Books.

Leder, M. (2001). *My life in Stalinist Russia: An American woman looks back.* Bloomington: Indiana University Press.

Lichtenstein, N. (2002). *State of the union: A century of American labor.* Princeton, NJ: Princeton University Press.

Lieberman, M. (2000). *The teacher unions: How they sabotage educational reform and why.* San Francisco: Encounter Books.

Ling, P. (1992). *America and the automobile: Technology, reform, and social change.* Manchester, UK: Manchester University Press.

Lipman, P. (1997). Restructuring in context: A case study of teacher participation and the dynamics of ideology, race, and power. *American Educational Research Journal,* 34 (1), 3–37.

Lovell, D. (1988). *Marx's proletariat: The making of a myth.* New York: Routledge Press.

Lukes, S. (1973). *Individualism.* New York: Harper & Row.

Lynch, F. (2002). *The diversity machine: The drive to change the "white male workplace."* New Brunswick, NJ: Transaction Publishers.

Maalouf, A. (2001). *In the name of identity: Violence and the need to belong.* New York: Arcade Press.

MacEwan, A. (1999). *Neo-liberalism or democracy: Economic strategy, markets, and alternatives for the 21st century.* New York: St. Martin's Press.

Madaus, G. (1990). The Distortion of teaching and testing: High-Stakes testing and instruction. *Peabody Journal of Education,* 65 (3), 29–46.

Maeroff, G. (1988). *The empowerment of teachers: Overcoming the crisis of confidence.* New York: Teachers College Press.

Mandel, E. (1973). *An introduction to Marxist economic theory.* New York: Pathfinder Press.

Mann, D. (1983). The impact of IMPACT II, *Teachers College Record,* 84 (4), 837–870.

Marcuse, H. (1985 [1958]). *Soviet Marxism: A critical analysis.* New York: Columbia University Press.

Marx, K. & Engels, F. (1977 [1848]). *Selected Writi*ngs. The communist manifesto, pp. 221–247. Oxford, UK: Oxford University Press.

Maslow, A. (1976). *The farther reaches of human nature.* New York: Penguin Books.

McLaren, P. (2000). *Che Guevara, Paulo Freire, and the pedagogy of revolution.* New York: Rowman Press.

McLaren, P. & Farahmandpur, R. (2000). Reconsidering Marx in post-Marxist times: A requiem for postmodernism. *Educational Researcher*, 29 (3), 25–33.

McNeil, L. (2000). *Contradictions of school reform: Educational costs of standardized testing*. New York: Routledge Press.

Menand, L. (2001). *The metaphysical club*. New York: Farrar, Straus & Giroux.

Meredith, M. (2002). *Our votes, our guns: Robert Mugabe and the tragedy of Zimbabwe*. New York: Public Affairs Press.

Merriman, J. (1996). *A history of modern Europe: From the renaissance to the present*. New York: Yale University Press.

Meyer, J. & Rowan, B. (1978). The structure of educational organizations. In M. Meyer (Ed.), *Environments and organizations*, 78–109. San Francisco: Jossey Bass.

Mill, J. (1999 [1848]). *Principles of political economy*. New York: Oxford University Press.

Miller, D. (1989). *Market, state, and community: Theoretical foundations of market socialism*. Oxford, UK: Oxford University Press.

Miller, R. (1995). *Educational freedom for a democratic society: A critique of national educational goals, standards, and curriculum*. Brandon, VT: Great Ideas in Education Press.

Mirel, J. (1994). School reform unplugged: The Bensenville new American school project. *American Educational Research Journal*, 31 (3), 481–518.

Mollat, M. (1986). *The poor in the middle ages: An essay in social history*. New Haven: Yale University Press.

Mory, E. & Salisbury, D. (1992). *School restructuring: The critical element of total system design*. Paper presented at the annual American Educational Research Association.

Muncey, D. & McQuillan, P. (1992). The dangers of assuming consensus for change. In G. Hess, Jr. (Ed.), *Empowering teachers and parents: School restructuring through the eyes of anthropologists*. Westport, CT: Greenwood Press.

Murphy, J. (1991). *Restructuring schools: Capturing and assessing the phenomena*. New York: Teachers College Press.

Murphy, M. (1990). *Blackboard unions the AFT and the NEA, 1900–1980*. Ithaca, NY: Cornell University Press.

Myers, M. (1986). When research does not help teachers. *American Educator*, 10 (2), 18–26.

Nash, G., Crabtree, C. & Dunn, R. (1997). *History on trial: Culture wars and the teaching of the past*. New York: A.A. Knopf.

Nietzsche, F. (1968). *The portable Nietzsche*. New York: Viking Press.

Nisbet, R. (1990). *The quest for community: A study in the ethics of order and freedom*. San Francisco: Institute for Contemporary Studies.

Nussbuam, M. (1996). *For love of country: Debating the limits of patriotism*. Boston: Beacon Press.

Nye, D. (1990). *Electrifying America: Social meanings of a new technology, 1880–1940*. Cambridge: MIT Press.

Oaks, J. (1995). *Keeping track: How schools structure inequality*. New Haven: Yale University Press.

Olson, L. (2001). *Freedom's daughters: The unsung heroines of the civil rights movement from 1830 to 1970*. New York: Scribner Press.

Onore, C. & Lester, N. (1993). *Changing schools by acting as if*. Paper presented at the annual American Educational Research Association.

Pakalov, V. (1993). *Lives on the edge: Single mothers and their children in the other America.* Chicago: University of Chicago Press.

Palmer, R. (1965). *A history of the modern world.* New York: Knopf Press.

Pateman, C. (1970). *Participation in democratic theory.* Cambridge: Cambridge University Press.

Pattillo-McCoy, M. (1999). *Black picket fences: Privilege and peril among the black middle class.* Chicago: University of Chicago Press.

Payne, R. (1995). *Poverty: A framework for understanding and working with students and adults from poverty.* Baytown, TX: RFT Publishing.

Peck, M. (1987). *A different drum: Community making and peace.* New York: Simon & Schuster.

Peterson, R. (1993). Creating a school that honors the traditions of a culturally diverse student body: La Escuela Fratney. In G. Smith (Ed.), *Public schools that work*, pp. 45–69. New York: Routledge Press.

Pinar, W., Reynolds, W., Slattery, P., & Taubman, P. (1995). *Understanding curriculum: An introduction to the study of historical and contemporary curriculum discourses.* New York: Peter Lang Press.

Pink, W. & Hyde, A. (1991). *Effective staff development for school change.* Norwood, NJ: Ablex Press.

Pipes, R. (1990). *The Russian revolution.* New York: Knopf.

Pipes, R. (1995). *Russia under the Bloshevik regime.* New York: Vintage Books.

Potter, J. (1974). *The American economy between the world wars.* New York: Wiley Press.

Postman, N. & Weingartner, C. (1969). *Teaching as a subversive activity.* New York: Delacorte Press.

Quantz, R., Rogers, J., & Dantley, M. (1991). Rethinking transformative leadership: Towards democratic reform of schools. *Journal of Education*, 173 (3), 96–118.

Rajchman, J. (1985). *Michel Foucault: The freedom of philosophy.* New York: Columbia University Press.

Ravitch, D. (2000). *Left back: A century of failed school reforms.* New York: Simon & Schuster.

Ravitch, D. & Finn, C. (1989). *What do our 17-year-olds know: A report on the first national assessment of history and literature.* New York: Harper Collins.

Rawls, J. (2001). *Justice as fairness: A restatement.* Cambridge, MA: Harvard University Press.

Reigeluth, C. (1987). The search for meaningful reform: A third wave educational system. *Journal of Instructional Development*, 10 (4), 3–14.

Rikowski, G. (1996). Left alone: End time for Marxist educational theory. *British Journal of Sociology of Education*, 17 (4), 415–452.

Roemer, M. (1991). What we talk about when we talk about school reform. *Harvard Educational Review*, 61 (4), 434–448.

Rorty, R. (1989). *Contingency, irony, and solidarity.* New York: Cambridge University Press.

Rorty, R. (1998). *Achieving our country.* Cambridge, MA: Harvard University Press.

Rorty, R. (1999). *Philosophy and social hope.* New York: Penguin Books.

Rosen, R. (2001). *The world split open: How the modern women's movement changed America.* New York: Penguin Books.

Sachs, J. & Logan, L. (1990). Control or development? A study of inservice education, *Journal of Curriculum Studies*, 22 (5), 473–481.

Sarason, S. (1971). *The culture of the school and the problem of change.* Boston: Allyn & Bacon, Inc.

Sarason, S. (1990). *The predictable failure of educational reform.* San Francisco: Jossey-Bass.

Sartre, J. (1956). *Being and nothingness: An essay on phenomenological ontology.* New York: Philosophical Library.

Schneirov, R. (1998). *Labor and urban politics: Class conflict and the origins of modern liberalism in Chicago, 1864–97.* Chicago: University of Illinois Press.

Schumacher, E. (1973). *Small is beautiful: Economic as if people mattered.* New York: Harper & Row.

Sen, A. (1984). *Poverty and famines: An essay on entitlement and deprivation.* New York: Oxford University Press.

Sen, A. (1992). *Inequality reexamined.* Cambridge, MA: Harvard University Press.

Sen, A. (2000). *Development as freedom.* New York: Anchor Books.

Sennett, R. (1977). *The fall of public man.* New York: Alfred Knopf.

Shank, B. (1994). Must schools of social work be freestanding? Yes. *Journal of Social Work Education*, 30 (3), 273–294.

Shannon, P. (1987). Commercial reading materials, a technological ideology, and the deskilling of teachers. *Elementary School Journal*, 87 (3), 309–329.

Shannon, P. (1998). *Reading poverty.* Portsmouth, NH: Heinemann Press.

Shepard, L. & Doughty, K. (1991, April). *Effects of high-stakes testing on instruction.* Paper presented at the American Educational Research Association and the National Council on Measurement in Education meeting.

Shor, I. (1992). *Culture wars: School and society in the conservative restoration.* Chicago: University of Chicago Press.

Silberman, C. (1970). *Crisis in the classroom: The remaking of American education.* New York: Random House.

Sklar, M. (1988). *The corporate reconstruction of American capitalism, 1890–1916: The market, the law, and politics.* New York: Cambridge University Press.

Skulnick, R. (2004). *What's your sign: A study of adolescent culture.* Doctoral dissertation, Bloomington, IN: Indiana University.

Sleeter, C. & Grant, C. (1999). *Making choices for multicultural education: Five approaches to race, class, and gender.* Upper Saddle River, NJ: Merrill Press.

Smith, A. (1991 [1776]). *Wealth of nations.* Buffalo, NY: Prometheus Books.

Smith, D. (1987). *The everyday world as problematic: A feminist sociology.* Boston: Northeastern University Press.

Smith, G. (1993). *Public schools that work: Creating community.* New York: Routledge.

Smyth, J. (1993). *A socially critical view of the self-managing school.* London: Falmer Press.

Solo, R. (2000). *Economic organizations and social systems.* Ann Arbor: University of Michigan Press.

Soltys, D. (1997). *Education for decline: Soviet vocational and technical schooling from Khrushchev to Gorbachev.* Toronto: University of Toronto Press.

Soros, G. (2002). *On globalization.* New York: Public Affairs.

Spradley, J. (1979). *The ethnographic interview.* New York: Rinehart & Winston.

Spring, J. (1989). *The sorting machine revisited: National educational policy since 1945.* New York: Longman.

Staggenborg, S. (1998). *Gender, family, and social movements.* Thousand Oaks: Pine Forge Press.

Stefancic, J. & Delgado, R. (1996). *No mercy: How conservative think tanks and foundations changed America's social agenda.* Philadelphia: Temple University Press.

Storrs, L. (2000). *Civilizing capitalism: The National Consumers' League, women's activism, and labor standards in the New Deal era.* Chapel Hill: University of North Carolina Press.

Sulla, N. (1998, April). *Maximizing the effectiveness of external consultants in the educational reform agenda.* Paper presented at the Annual American Educational Research Association meeting.

Sunstein, C. (1997). *Free markets and social justice.* New York: Oxford University Press.

Symcox, L. (2002). *Whose history? The struggle for national standards in American classrooms.* New York: Teachers College Press.

Talbot, D. & Crow, G. (1998, April). *When the school changed, did I get a new job? Principals' role conceptions in a restructuring context.* Paper presented at the annual American Educational Research Association.

Tang, T., Toai, D., & Chanoff, D. (2000). *A Viet Cong memoir: An inside account of the Vietnam war and its aftermath.* Bloomington: Indiana University Press.

Teele, S. (2000). *Rainbows of intelligence: Exploring how students learn.* Thousand Oaks, CA: Corwin Press.

Trotsky, L. (1972 [1937]). *The revolution betrayed: What is the Soviet Union and where is it going.* Sheffield, UK: Mehring Books.

Urban, W. (1982). *Why teachers organized.* Detroit: Wayne State University Press.

Valencia, R. (1997). *The evolution of deficit thinking: Educational thought and practice.* New York: Falmer Press.

Vinson, K., Gibson, R., & Ross, W. (2001). High-stakes testing and standardization: The threat to authenticity. *Progressive Perspectives, 3* (2), 1–13.

Viroli, M. (1995). *For love of country: An essay on patriotism and nationalism.* Oxford, UK: Clarendon Press.

Wallerstein, I. (1995). *After liberalism.* New York: The New Press.

Watts, G. & Castle, S. (1992). *The time dilemma in school restructuring.* Paper presented at the annual American Educational Research Association meeting.

Webb, S. (1901). *English progress towards social democracy.* London: Fabian Society Press.

Weber, M. (1998 [1946]). *The Protestant ethic and the spirit of capitalism.* Los Angeles: Roxbury Publishing Co.

Weick, K. (1988). Educational organizations as loosely coupled systems. In A. Westoby (Ed.), *Culture and power in educational organizations.* Philadelphia: Open University Press.

Weis, L. & Fine, M. (1993). *Beyond silenced voices: Class, race and gender in United States schools.* Albany: State University of New York Press.

White, P. (1992). Teacher empowerment under "ideal" school-site autonomy. *Educational Evaluation and Policy Analysis, 14* (1), 69–82.

Wiebe, R. (1967). *The search for order, 1877–1920.* New York: Hill & Wang Press.

Williams, R. (1977). *Marxism and literature.* London: Oxford University Press.

Willis, G. (1999). *A necessary evil: A history of American distrust of government*. New York: Simon & Schuster.

Wlodzimierz, B. & Laski, K. (1989). *From Marx to the market: Socialism in search of an economic system*. Oxford, UK: Clarendon Press.

Wolfe, A. (1998). *One nation after all: What middle-class Americans really think*. New York: Vintage Press.

Wood, D. (2003). *The challenges of creating an authentic collegial context for change*. Paper presented at the annual American Educational Research Association meeting.

Wood, E. (1972). *Mind and politics: An approach to the meaning of liberal and socialist individualism*. Berkeley: University of California Press.

Wood, G. (1992). *Schools that work: America's most innovative public education programs*. New York: Dutton Press.

Wood, E. & Foster, J. (1997). *In defense of history: Marxism and the postmodern agenda*. New York: Monthly Review Press.

Woodward, A. (1986). Over-programmed materials: Taking the teacher out of teaching. *American Educator*, 10 (1), 22–25.

Yankelovich, D. (1999). *The magic of dialogue: Transforming conflict into cooperation*. New York: Simon & Schuster.

Yendol-Silva, D. (2003). *In search of the perfect storm: Understanding how learning communities create power within an era of intense accountability*. Paper presented at the annual American Educational Research Association.

Yukl, G. (1994). *Leadership in organizations*. Englewood Cliffs, NJ: Prentice-Hall.

Zakaria, F. (2003). *The future of freedom: Illiberal democracy at home and abroad*. New York: Norton Press.

Zeichner, K. (1986). Social and ethical dimensions of reform in teacher education. In J. Hoffman & S. Edwares (Eds.), *Reality and reform in clinical teacher education*, 87–107. New York: Random House.

Zimmerman, J. (2002). *Whose America: Culture wars in the public schools*. Cambridge, MA: Harvard University Press.

Zou, Y. & Trueba, T. (1998). *Ethnic identity and power: Cultural contexts of political action in school and society*. Albany: State University of New York Press.

Zweigenhaft, R. & Domhoff, W. (1991). *Blacks in the white establishment? A study of race and class in America* New Haven: Yale University Press.

Zweigenhaft, R. & Domhoff, W. (1998). *Diversity in the power elite: Have women and minorities reached the top?* New Haven: Yale University Press.

INDEX

academic: skills, 16; standards, 20
accountability, 15, 16, 90; agenda, 17
Adelman, N., 91
administrators, xviii, 21, 70–74
Allington, R., 16
Allman, P., 8
Althusser, L., 8
Ambrose, S., 7
American Educational Research
    Association, 89
American Enterprise Institute, 7
ancestral heritages, 2; African, 20, 123;
    African American, 12, 35, 60, 62,
    75–76, 106, 111, 124; Anglo-
    Americans, 89, 123; Anglo-Saxon
    Protestant tradition in Europe, 20;
    Asian, 12, 123; Asian American, 20;
    Euro-American, 19, 60, 106, 111;
    identity, 18; males, 19, 81; *See also*
    class; tradition and identity, 19;
    Hispanic, 62, 123; Irish, 123; Italian,
    123; Jewish, 20, 123; Latinos, 12
Andersen, R., 7
Anderson, G., 29, 55–56, 74
antisemitism, 125
Anyon, J., 49, 65–66
Apple, M., ix, xiv, 1, 3, 14, 15, 20, 47,
    121
aristocracy, 11, 32, 34; power of, 33; *See
    also* power
Armstrong, T., 91
Aronowitz, S., 8
Aronson, R., 2, 123
Association of Curriculum and
    Supervision, the, 27
authenticity, 74–75, 77–78; through reci-
    procity, 78; *See also* reciprocity
autobiographical scholarship, 37, 116–17

autonomy, x, xiv–xv, 40; as a state of
    power, 53; organizational, as a state of
    mind, 52; relative economic, 8; *See also*
    economics; school, 37, 39–41, 43–46,
    48, 51–52, 55, 80, 85; *See also* school
Avrich, P., 5, 123
Ayers, W., 124

Bakhtin, Mikhail, 100
Baldwin, J., 24
Banaszak, L., 5, 35
Banathy, B., 108
Barber, B., 1, 3, 7, 10, 14, 25, 123
Barker, J., 55, 74
Baron, D., 28
Barth, R., 40, 56
Bates, S., 94
Beare, H., 74
Beck, L., 39
Belcher, M., 28
Bell, D., 8, 18
Bellah, R., 24
Bennett, William, 7, 94
Berlinger, D., 2, 124
Biddle, B., 2, 124
Binder, A., 18
Bintz, W., 28
Bismark, 35
Black, D., 36
Blank, R., 123
Blase, J., 29, 39
Blau, J., 3, 36
Bloom, L., 65, 100
Bodnar, J., 25
Bonchek, S., 28
bourgeoisie, 1, 9, 11–16, 18, 20, 26,
    32–35, 81, 89, 117, 122–23; petty, 13,
    17; *See also* class